# Advanced Obedience

## *Easier Than You Think*

## JOEL M. McMAINS

BOOK HOUSE

New York

Maxwell Macmillan Canada
Toronto

Maxwell Macmillan International
New York   Oxford   Singapore   Sydney

Howell Book House
Macmillan Publishing Company
866 Third Avenue
New York, NY 10022

Maxwell Macmillan Canada, Inc.
1200 Eglinton Avenue East
Suite 200
Don Mills, Ontario M3C 3N1

Macmillan Publishing Company is part of the Maxwell Communication Group of Companies.

**3 3113 01299 4598**

Library of Congress Cataloging-in-Publication Data

McMains, Joel M.
Advanced obedience—easier than you think / Joel M. McMains.
p.   cm.
Includes bibliographical references and index.
ISBN 0-87605-522-6
1. Dogs—Obedience trials.   2. Dogs—Training.   I. Title.
SF425.7.M36        1993              92-38628
636.7'0887—dc20

Macmillan books are available at special discounts for bulk purchases for sales promotions, premiums, fund-raising, or educational use. For details, contact:

Special Sales Director
Macmillan Publishing Company
866 Third Avenue
New York, NY 10022

10 9 8 7 6 5 4 3 2 1

Printed in the United States of America

*In memory of my German Shepherd Dog, Smokey:*
*June 19, 1982–November 3, 1991.*
*Much of what I know about* Canis familiaris
*I learned from him; or, I should say, he taught me.*

# Contents

# Preface

THIS BOOK takes up where its predecessor, *Dog Logic—Companion Obedience,* leaves off. More than a continuation of the first text, the two are as one; kin, rather than just friends. Many of the techniques described in this book derive from *Dog Logic* foundational principles and lessons.

To maintain a broad perspective, *Dog Logic* and the books that follow it are not based upon American Kennel Club, Schutzhund or other competition requirements. This manual includes a run-for-the-ribbons section, as healthy competition is a meaningful and fulfilling promotion of the human-canine relationship. Still, training for intrinsic worth is preferable to concentrating on how the work might be used. For instance, teaching scent discrimination (retrieving a trainer-scented object) to a "pet-only" dog might seem pointless if one doesn't intend to compete in the AKC Utility class, which requires the exercise's performance. But scent training has value for its own sake. It allows a dog to hone his abilities while acknowledging his unique gift for scent identification. Such training not only allows a dog to be a dog, it validates and rejoices in his essence. (It's also a blessing when a trainer accidentally drops his car keys in a foot of wet snow.) As stated in *Dog Logic*'s preface, "Competition is best viewed as but one possible expression of a thoroughly schooled dog, not as an end in itself."

If this is your initial foray into the realm of upper-level work, or even if you've journeyed this road many times, an illusion needs dispelling—e.g., advanced work is harder, more complex, and more taxing than teaching the basics. That's the myth. The reality is that it's often the other way around.

The very existence of concepts like *basic* and *advanced* can suggest that any work beyond rudimentary lessons is inherently more difficult, in understanding, application and complexity. But dog training is dog training, and there's little variance in difficulty from one level to another. Consider scent discrimination, mentioned earlier. From human perspective the work seems astoundingly arduous, even mysterious. That's because you and I don't have *Canis familiaris*'s scenting capability. Yet to a dog, the ability to discriminate among scents is easy; it's natural, certainly more so than many conventional obedience exercises, and therefore more easily taught.

A sound dog, bonded to the human pack leader and well-schooled in novice obedience, presents few problems during advanced work. Given a solid relationship and a sound basic obedience foundation, postgraduate instruction is often easier because trainer and trainee have already cleared so many hurdles. The dog has learned that the trainer is in charge, that he or she has things to teach. Communication has been established, status has been defined.

The key to advanced, rapport-based training is that by the time a person reaches this level, either he has something going with his dog, or he probably never will without considerable restructuring. Given sound bonding, though, the lessons are easily absorbed, and much time and effort is saved.

Our culture promotes instant (if wanting), orchestrated results, from fast food to what passes for justice. "I want it now!" mind-sets are commonplace. Newcomers to training can (subconsciously, at least) expect immediate, Rin-Tin-Tin effects from their efforts at dog training. It doesn't work that way, though. A good dog learns as quickly as he's able. He's driven to please not just himself, but his human partner as well. Though training doesn't require great amounts of daily time, several weeks are needed for the cultivation and ripening of bonding, upon which rapport-based training rests. A dog needs time to develop trust, to build confidence, in himself and in his owner.

Another stumbling block to upper-level obedience occurs with dogs who perform passably at elementary work but fall apart at advanced levels. Seldom the animal's fault, this is often due to incomplete conditioning. Pooch was shown several obedience functions—heel, sit, stay, and so forth—but the notion that he must respond to command despite nearby happenings was never made clear. Result: habitual faulty concentration leading to obedience lapses during stages demanding more prolonged concentration. Remember: An obligation you have toward your student when you take over the *Alpha* function—that is, when you assume the parental role, essentially becoming your pet's surrogate mom and dad—is that fairness demands you explain all rules as clearly as possible. To do less is to abuse the dog and to violate the relationship's covenants.

In keeping with that counsel, master the content of chapter 1, "Reinforcement Techniques," prior to dealing with new material. Until your companion does well with enhancements applicable to his environment, and until he's reliable around appropriate distractions, he isn't ready to progress. To presume otherwise is to unfairly hold the dog accountable. It is also to attempt to build upon a shaky foundation. Then the question becomes not, "Will the obedience break down?", but *"When* will the obedience break down?" Experience answers, "Probably in situations where the owner needs it most."

Finally, keep in mind an essential theme of my training/writing philosophy: Like Eliot's cat, only the dog knows his own deep and inscrutable singular Name. As written in *Dog Logic*'s preface, "[The book] is a work of opinion and conjecture: the only ones who can finally know are the dogs themselves." I remind you of this because the farther up any ladder one ascends, the greater the need to maintain balance, maintain perspective.

# Acknowledgments

---

I'M BEHOLDEN to many who have assisted in this book's completion: Ron Flath, Jo Sykes, Roger Davidson, Darryl Dockstader, Sharon Michael, Jim Robinson, Dick Moore, and most of all, H.P. I especially thank Seymour Weiss of Howell Book House, whose many talents have greatly aided my writing efforts in the *Dog Logic* series.

*Skill is the arrow,
desire, the bow.*

# SECTION I

# Beyond Companion Obedience

# 1

# Reinforcement Techniques

---

## PART I—DISTRACTION PROOFING

Distractions are stimuli that may entice a dog to break from command. Proofing is exposing pooch to distractions. The purpose is to teach the animal in a controlled setting that he must obey your commands despite happenings nearby.

This section doesn't outline every distractive mechanism I've ever used—that would be a book in itself. My intent is to characterize various strategies to impart the feel, the flavor of conditioning, to help you devise additional lessons.

### Perspective

The first time a person works his or her pet around heavy distractions—especially away from home—can be a sobering moment. Many a good dog is less reliable on the outside than when in his own backyard. The score can quickly read DISTRACTIONS 10–POOCH 0. While such an outcome simply accents the obvious—the trainer is correct in working on distraction proofing—a broader message is that it may be a good time to review a vital training element: patience.

Outsiders often wonder at professional trainers' consistent patience. Owners can sometimes ruffle a trainer's feathers, but dogs—hardly ever. A learned attribute, it's more a product of awareness than rehearsal. One can practice mechanical training skills—leash technique, heeling style, ring-handling procedures and so on—honing them toward reflexive accuracy. But one can't "practice" patience. The closest a person can come to that is through adoption of a "bite-your-tongue" posture mislabeled as patience. Trouble can then arise from the fact that repressing anger isn't only unhealthy, it's unrealistic. Ultimately the cannon explodes, usually catching pooch in its line of fire.

True patience comes through realization of two points. First, dogs (like people) invariably do their best. They goof now and then, yes, but that was their best at that moment. Trainers know this, and that some dogs are more distraction-sensitive than others. A patient trainer doesn't stymie a dog's best efforts today, blocking the animal's best from getting better tomorrow. Knowledgeable trainers don't lock animals into shame cycles. They understand that when a dog bungles an assignment, it means only that their job—teaching—is unfinished.

Second, frustration born of surprise can lead to anger when weeks of training seem to come apart around distractions. The explanation for this obedience breakdown extends from a point made in *Dog Logic:* "Most canines don't generalize certain types of learned behaviors."* The example given is that a dog who knows ". . . to Sit on command, to hold a Sit-Stay, to Sit automatically at Heel, and to Sit automatically in front of and facing you after a Recall" won't necessarily "Sit!" from the Down position without further teaching. He would "were you training an animal possessing human thought patterns, but . . . dogs simply don't process information that way." "Sit!" calls for downward movement of the *derrière*, and that's hard for pooch to do when he's lying on the ground.

The parallel is that a dog who has learned to perform many command behaviors in one setting usually doesn't—can't—reflexively apply his knowledge to greatly different settings. He has to be shown how to do that. Though the trainer's commands are unchanged, the context in which they're given is so different that a canine may view them as night and day. Humans tend to see sameness in backyard heeling and heeling near a busy schoolyard, heeling being the common denominator. To a dog, though, the difference in pattern is profound.

*Dog Logic,* chapter 10, p. 158.

Perhaps you've experienced these insights. If so, they've gifted you with that special serenity that obviates any need for anger. If not, be attentive and your dog will reinforce them for you. Remember that two beings are involved in pooch's education, and be patient with both of them.

## Guidelines

Taking every dog through every step isn't mandatory, but do so with animals whose working environments are highly stressful. Still, if your pal is primarily a house pet, there's no point in working him near the train yards as the 4:40 freight rumbles through. Condition at a dog's real-world level, always.

During initial exposures to distractions, begin with familiar basics. Using Stay as an example, start with brief, short-distance, on-leash Stays, not prolonged, Out-of-sight work. As conditioning implies higher-stress situations than those to which your dog is accustomed, start with work in which he's confident. Complicated obedience can be added as you progress together.

No distraction should appear threatening. Your dog was born with a drive to protect himself as well as you, and to contrive a setting intended to counter that drive would be unsettling in the extreme.

Lastly, recognize that during distraction training, you know what's coming, distraction-wise—as well as what's expected—but pooch doesn't. That can ready two traps. First, an attitude of, "This'll cause the dog to mess up," may prove self-fulfilling by transmitting the expectation along the leash. Maintain positive thoughts. Second, should your student forsake obedience in response to a distraction, don't respond with $n^{th}$-degree compulsion. Force is appropriate once a dog knows the rules, but not until then. For instance, your pet may not realize that he's supposed to maintain the Heel position as a stranger approaches. Instinct drives him to investigate. That's not disobedience; it's part of being a dog. Had the animal known his action was wrong, that it wasn't what you wanted, he wouldn't have done it.

Patience.

## The Darnedest Things Can Disrupt Obedience

The following scenarios deal with requiring that a dog be obedient around strangers. Bear in mind there's a difference between the two of you approaching a stranger, and a stranger approaching the two of you. Because the latter is potentially threatening in pooch's eyes, your helpers must behave normally.

Heel toward a person unknown to your dog, but who is actually in cahoots with you. Stop, perhaps shake hands, and visit briefly. Your pet should do an Automatic Sit and remain in that position, but unless you've conditioned for such events, he may not. Be ready to block him from advancing at full sniff toward your helper.*

Turn up the heat on this exercise by having your assistant bring his dog (assuming both animals have sufficient training not to instigate a fight). Each should maintain the Sit position while you and your helper converse.

To make this and similar conditioning more effective, use different helpers. Otherwise, a dog can learn he must comport himself properly only in the presence of a particular individual.

Try this one. As your pet sits automatically during heeling, bend over and tie your shoelace, or sit next to him. It's probable the dog will abandon his sit since changes in your pattern of behavior affect his.

A variation is to heel toward a park bench or the like, command, "Platz"† (or "Sit"), as you arrive, then rest yourself on the object momentarily. Likely as not, when you sit your dog will presume he needn't remain in the commanded position. Similarly, when you stand, the animal will probably stand, even though you've given no command cancelling the "Platz" (or "Sit") directive.

Here's another. Have a stranger to your pet play the role of a jogger or a bicyclist passing you at a realistic distance. The helper shouldn't come directly at you—that could appear threatening.

### "Me? Heel Across *That?*"

Objects, as well as people, can suspend obedience. Try heeling across a see-through, metal grate, the type often found in city sidewalks. When first encountering the strange surface, your companion may wish

---

*Don't isolate pooch from this meeting. That could make him feel he doesn't belong. Prior to leaving the helper, introduce your pet—using his name—so he sees you're neither shutting him out nor belittling his status.

†For reasons given in chapter 7 of *Dog Logic,* I recommend the use of two German commands, "Fuss" and "Platz." Fuss means "foot" and rhymes with "loose." *Platz* translates as "spot," or "place," and rhymes with "lots."

to explore it briefly. Ideally he'd trot right across the thing—and with familiarization he will—but during a first experience he likely won't.

If pooch shies away from the foreign surface, *don't* respond with force. The problem is fear, not disobedience, and pressure in such a situation is not only inhumane, it exacerbates fear and breeds distrust. Command, "Stay," and step onto the grate yourself, paying it no attention. This can demonstrate that neither of you is going to fall into a bottomless pit.* Then summon your pet—kneel and encourage him, if need be—presenting a food bit as he arrives. The chewy is neither bribe nor reward. Its purpose is to distract from the distraction, to allow pooch a breather emotionally. Once he's on the unfamiliar surface, pet the animal. Then heel away, marveling at how well he's doing. Don't put him on a second grate today. One success is sufficient for now.

An important conditioning element is that—like any training period—you mustn't allow a session to end in failure. If you start a procedure, plan to stay with it until success results. Otherwise the lesson's message to your partner, in the above illustration, is that he's right to avoid such strange places, and trying to get him onto such a footing later becomes that much harder.

However, should pooch react with outright paranoia toward a grating, settle for heeling near the surface a few times. Come closer the following day, stepping onto the grate yourself. A day later, get the dog onto the object. You'll succeed if patience and understanding are your watchwords.

### The Closed-Gate or Closed-Door Ploy

An excellent heeling-distraction technique is heeling toward a *closed* gate or door through which the two of you have passed many times before, and when you arrive, stop. Don't open or even reach for the latch. I bet pooch blows the Automatic Sit, responding instead by standing in place. It's his patterned nature to expect you to open the gate or door as before, and he's probably learned there's no need to sit because you'll both be moving again shortly. If your worker does skip the Auto-Sit, out-and-out disobedience isn't the problem. He's yet to internalize the Auto-Sit's exactitude, and it's your job to clarify that responsibility.

---

*Generally, in situations regarding new people, places or things, if you treat it as no big deal, neither will your dog.

**The Open-Gate or Open-Door Ploy**

A variation has the trainer heeling toward an open gate or door, but turning away from the portal at the last second. The turn is more effective when made as a right- or an about-turn. A left turn tends to body-guide a dog instead of requiring that he maintain handler awareness without benefit of subtle cueing.

Should your trainee anticipate by scooting ahead, take care not to whack his head or drag him against a gatepost or door jamb for trying to out-think you. One text I've encountered recommends a good jolt to the errant animal's belfry, but that's way too much. It's abuse. It's also risky in terms of injury. A collar pop for lost concentration is adequate correction.

A similar setup is to heel toward an upright post, causing your companion to have to walk by it closely enough that he may try to go around it (i.e., momentarily placing the object between the two of you). Again, if your companion starts to go around the post, don't leash-drag him across the structure. Use a leash-pop correction.

**Crowds**

For these lessons you'll need the help of a few people not well known to your pet. Half a dozen willing souls are enough, but more—up to twenty—would be better. Have your helpers stand three to four feet apart, and form a corridor ten feet wide. Don't take your dog from person to person as a form of introduction, but make certain each helper knows the animal's name.*

The following format is described in terms of heeling but it can also be used with Stays, Recalls, and, later, Retrieving. On-leash your pet through the corridor, never coming closer to anyone than four feet. The group should pay you and your dog little mind during this initial pass, perhaps chatting among themselves. During the second walk-through, the helpers should call your dog in normal voice, not by name, but, "Hey—c'mere, pup, c'mere." During the next pass they should continue to call, emphasizing attempts at contact by patting their legs suggestively and by kneeling and clapping their hands. During the final trip the group should use the dog's name when calling, as in, "C'mere, [dog's name], c'mere."

---

*Don't use family members or close friends for this conditioning. A dog should respond when called by a family member. Constraining that response can inspire a distrustful, nervous attitude.

The phases may be covered during one session, or they may take several. It depends on your pet's reactions to the group's efforts. Should pooch be attracted to a caller, hold conditioning at that level until the animal maintains attention on you despite distractions. Add "No" to any corrections, accompanied by patting your left leg or chest for emphasis.

After each session, the group should meet and pet your dog. If this isn't done, the animal can learn distrust of strangers. Paranoia isn't the lesson here: trust in you is.

### If You're Training More than One Dog

Use him, or her, or them. Require one or more to Sit- or Down-Stay while you work or play nearby with another. Then swap animals, commanding the dog you were working, "Stay."

### Here a Tidbit, There a Tidbit

Have a helper drop some golfball-sized hamburger bits in an area you'll soon heel through. If a family member helps you, he or she should wear rubber gloves so not to scent the meat with notions of "Dinner time!" That would be unfair. Yes, this exercise is advisable for potential hunters and search-and-rescue candidates. You're going to *heel* through the area, and "Fuss" is "Fuss." The command doesn't mean, "Heel, unless you find something else to do."

### Gunfire

If you plan for your dog to work near gunfire, condition near local gun-club ranges during their practices. If no such organization is nearby, perhaps friends can be enlisted to sight-in their artillery while you train. Start a reasonable distance from the noise, coming closer as your pet develops steadiness. If your dog becomes anxious, marked by lost and unrecoverable concentration, pronounced skittishness, excessive panting, freezing in place, and so on, start farther away. Should the problem persist, it's possible pooch's genetic predisposition will always prevent him from being steady around gunfire or similar noises.

### "Work in the Rain? Me? Surely You Jest!"

If that subtitle bespeaks your dog's attitude the first time you work him in a shower, your response should be, "No, I don't! Fuss!" If you

want obedience to be true in other than warm, sunny weather, inform your student before need arises.

Instead of waiting for a storm to blow through, make use of lawn sprinklers. Don't use the harsh-blast, rotating variety. That's a bit much. Fountain and oscillating types are better suited for the purpose. Be sure to towel your friend afterward.

### Remember: This Is a Dog You're Training

The following applies regardless of your pet's gender. If you've access to a bitch in season, work near her. No, don't walk your dog right up next to her and run him through various paces for half an afternoon. However, it is proper to work (*on leash*) briefly within several yards of this challenging distraction.

A variation is to locate a tree or post that neighborhood canines frequently anoint. Heel and do Recalls within a few feet of the object.

Some feel that such schemes expect too much from man's best friend. I strongly disagree. It's in high-stress environments that one needs reliable obedience most.

### Distractions Summary

The foregoing lessons condition for real-world situations a dog is likely to encounter. Sure, they're setups, but if done properly, pooch won't learn there's a difference between the staged and the authentic.

## PART II—CONCEPTUAL ENHANCEMENTS

This section presents methods designed to hone understanding of concepts already learned. To you and me the following drills are subtle variations on earlier lessons, but a dog's patterned makeup may cause him to see them as new material. Compulsion is inappropriate unless your efforts are met with bad-attitude resistance. Trainers don't correct until a dog knows the work. Amateurs might; trainers don't.

### Heel on Right

Teaching right-side heeling is *not* for competition animals until all titles have been earned. While off-side heeling may seem something of a taboo, teach it if the capability would offer a useful alternative.

Teaching right-side heeling is no harder than teaching conventional heeling. The only technique difference, other than everything being reversed, is the command: "Right" instead of "Fuss."

A need to anticipate is helping your companion adapt emotionally to the modification. His behaviorally patterned nature is of such depth that it may take a while before he feels comfortable in the new position. Praise often to show, "No, you aren't doing something wrong; that's the side I want you on for now."

Teach your dog to shift from one heeling position to the other while in motion. For example, while heeling pooch at your right side, he or she should respond to "Fuss" by ducking behind you to reappear in the conventional Heel position. Teach this by commanding, "Right," and—after a few paces—commanding, "Fuss," while lightly and suggestively tugging the leash leftward from behind your back.

## Recall Variants

You know the format of a Recall. After leaving your dog on a Stay, he responds to "Here" by coming to you, automatically sitting in front of and facing you upon arrival. That structure is fine for as far as it goes. It's right at home in the context of an obedience exhibition. In other than contrived scenarios, though, such patterned obedience can prove impractical at best.

For instance, if it were necessary to summon your friend while keeping your back to his line of approach, what would he do upon arrival? Ideally he'd come around in front of you and sit, but without practice the animal is more likely to arrive and manifest confusion about what to do next. Since a confused dog is by definition not under control, obedience can't be operating in such a situation. Here are some Recall modifiers for your postgraduate program.

Leave your student on a Sit- or Down-Stay, move away a few steps, assume a sitting or kneeling position, and call him. Will the dog sit upon arrival? Probably not. The situation is too altered. An extension is to call your dog, and—before he can cover the distance to you—vanish from sight. The next step is calling him *after* you've disappeared.*

Alteration of time can be an enhancement. Sit-Stay your dog, go to leash's end, face the animal and call, "Here." So far we've done nothing

---

*This step shouldn't be taken with competition animals until all titles requiring Out-of-Sight Stays have been earned.

new; we've merely put the dog in a Recall frame of mind. Now, repeat the exercise, but this time stand in place for thirty seconds prior to summoning your pet. The altered time factor—that is, not calling the dog soon after leaving him—may reveal that your co-worker's understanding of the Recall is not as thorough as you'd thought. He may come to you, but not without a moment's hesitation due to the broken pattern. The purpose, of course, is to demonstrate that it doesn't matter *when* you give a command. The important event is your command's occurrence.

Another enhancer is teaching your pet to come when called regardless what you're doing or which direction you happen to be facing. Rather than require he Sit in the classic front-and-facing position upon arrival, call, "Fuss" (instead of "Here"), and show him to come to the Heel position. To teach the concept, start by leaving your dog on a Sit-Stay and moving away ten feet. Keeping your back to him throughout the lesson, command, "Fuss," after you've been gone a few seconds. Begin walking forward at the same instant, the idea being to attract the animal through your motion, rather than through leash pressure. Initially slap your left leg when commanding, "Fuss." Praise, "Good Fuss," as your buddy comes alongside. Stop after a few steps, to remind the dog he should still Auto-Sit at heel.

Once pooch has the idea, which seldom takes more than three or four presentations, occasionally begin moving at other than a normal pace after summoning him. Sometimes run, other times walk slowly. As your companion adapts to these modifications, periodically call him to your side while remaining stationary. Then progress to calling the dog to heel while facing him.

Extend these Recall alterations by lengthening your starting distance over the next few sessions. Also, vary the elapsed time between leaving and calling your pet from a few seconds to a few minutes. The purpose for these adjustments is to clarify that it's your command that matters, not what you're doing when you give it.

Another practical variation is to teach your dog to join you at heel when *he's* already in motion, when you've not left him on a Stay. This is most useful when your friend is running around the yard, for example, and you suddenly need his presence.

Of course, some of these modifications can't effectively be made until the dog is reliable off-leash, and preferably off-collar. Chapter 4 covers both training levels.

## Finish Enhancements

Leave your partner on a Sit-Stay. Move to your right instead of forward, going as far as the six-foot leash allows. You should wind up several feet to your pet's right, facing in the same direction as he. After a few seconds, command, "Fuss," and pat your left leg invitingly. Praise, "Good Fuss," as your friend aligns in the Heel position. Remind, "Sit," if need be, as he may be somewhat befuddled by the new procedure. If the dog has difficulty with the lesson, shorten the starting distance. However, be aware that a beginning span of mere inches can prove as much of a problem as too far a range. Were you to start from six inches, for instance, the dog may respond to "Fuss" by remaining in place. He may not see such a narrow gap as signifying he's removed from the Heel position. His response might be, "Fuss? What do you mean? I'm already there." Obviously, in the face of this or similar confusion, force is improper. Communication is what's needed.

The next step is to leave pooch on a Sit-Stay, again moving a few steps right, but this time instead of facing the same direction as he when commanding, "Fuss," turn 180 degrees, thereby facing yourself in the *opposite* direction. Command, "Fuss." Your change of direction may cause the dog to expend more mental wattage than during the first Finish variant, but that's to the good of all concerned. The more you can cause a dog to think, the better a worker you'll ultimately have.

Another modification is to tell your pet, "Stay," and position yourself immediately to his left, in a mirror-image Heel position. When commanded, "Fuss," the dog may try to duck behind you to go to the Heel position, instead of taking the longer way around your front. Either is an acceptable response. Both bespeak a high degree of initiative, and as long as the end result is correct, such enterprise should be appreciated.

## Reverse Finish

Long after your companion has mastered the Finish itself, reinforce the Here concept by teaching the Reverse Finish. With the animal sitting at heel, Here tells him to step forward, turn right, and move to the front-and-facing position.

To teach this variant, first perform a couple of normal Recalls (but skip the Finish), the idea being to prepare pooch's mind for what's coming. Then, with your pet in the Heel position, command, "Here," and take a quick, long, heeling-like step forward with your left foot. Don't move your right foot. Though "Fuss" wasn't commanded, your trainee will probably step forward in response to leg movement. Quickly pull your left foot back and leash-turn the animal into the front-and-facing position. Praise "Good Here," as he sits. The procedure now becomes one of accompanying "Here" with progressively less foot movement.

## Enhancements Summary

The preceding ideas are by no means all that can be done to heighten understanding. Hopefully they'll suggest others for deepening comprehension. Should an idea occur to you, try it. Remember, though, that if problems arise with modified prior learning, disobedience is rarely the cause. The difficulty is usually confusion, often from inadvertently failing to link one training step with another. Then, of course, force is totally out of place. Further teaching is needed.

## Reflection

> *They are honest creatures,*
> *And they ne'er betray their masters, never fawn*
> *On any they love not.*
>
> Chief Justice Appleton (Maine)

15

Teaching the Stay hand signal.

# 2

# Hand Signals

---

**Pluses and Minuses**

A gentle way for trainer and trainee alike to ease into advanced obedience is via hand-signal work. It's simple material for the trainer, and most dogs learn hand signals easier and quicker than spoken commands. This is logical from canine perspective: dogs naturally communicate much and often through body language. Audible cues play a part in the animal world but to a lesser degree. As any knowledgeable breeder can attest, a dam's glance can abruptly moderate an exuberant puppy's rowdy behavior, and her pointed stare can stop him cold in his tracks.

A drawback to signal commands is that in settings other than AKC obedience trials and specialized working functions, their use isn't always practical for the average pet owner. A sudden need for obedience is often triggered by the unplanned, and that spawns a distractive, stressful environment. In the context of dog training, a corollary to Murphy's Law might be stated: *The likelihood that a dog won't be looking at the trainer when a signal is given increases with the degree of environmental stress the animal perceives.*

A second pitfall of signal work is that a handler can lapse in concentration and inadvertently send a cue. I've seen signal trainers unconsciously adjust eyeglasses, scratch an itch, alter posture, and so forth, and then wonder why the dog suddenly broke an obedience sequence.

That said, a positive aspect of signal work is heightened attention on the handler. A dog learns that the only way he can receive instructions is by keeping an eye on Number One. An even greater plus of signals is they heighten bonding, since the cues occur at a more intimate level. Dogs view them as more personal than verbal commands—everybody else doesn't get to hear. For that reason alone, owners of "pet only" dogs should teach hand signals. During high-stress, real-world situations, however, rely on verbal commands.

## Signal-Teaching Guidelines

Teach each hand signal only after pooch is adept at the work under voice command, so the animal has a sound to associate with the signal. When teaching signals, remain silent throughout the session (I'll mention exceptions as we go along). As commands are given in silence, so praise and correction should be nonverbal. Repeated switching between voice and signals during initial instruction can obscure the lesson. Introduce a signal only after running the dog through the exercise under verbal command first, the idea being to set up the animal's mind for the work. To ensure control, train on-leash unless otherwise directed.

## "What If He Didn't See Me?"

Once it's apparent that your dog has the idea, it's a major error to withhold a signal until he happens to glance your way. If you are about to give a signal, but just then your companion looks away, *do not wait* until he looks back before giving the silent command. The teacher decides when a command is to be given—not the student. Using Stay as an example, give the signal and leave normally. Should the dog also attempt to depart, having inattentively missed the signal, correct for the broken Stay and immediately exit again. If the animal seems confused, repeat the hand signal when leaving the second time. True, commands shouldn't be repeated, but when clarity of intent is on the line, theoretical ideals must defer to practical considerations.

## Stay (Sitting)

As the first Stay your dog learned was the Sit-Stay, it's preferable to begin with that position to introduce the Stay signal. The goals are threefold. First, to teach the Stay signal. Second, to show your pet that hand signals exist in concept. The third and perhaps most important

The hand signal for heeling.

Notice the slack leash during Recall teaching.

objective is to reinforce that he must keep his attention on you when working.

The Stay signal is taught in much the same manner as the "Stay" voice command. Begin with a verbally commanded Sit-Stay of short distance and brief duration. After returning to the Heel position, praise silently and—without moving pooch from his present location—give a palm-over-his-eyes Stay signal. Step away the same number of paces as before. Return after a few seconds, and praise silently. Communicate approval through brief petting, flashing the Stay signal, more quick petting, giving the signal again, and still more petting. Increase distance and duration of this silent Stay at the same rate for teaching the verbal Stay (see *Dog Logic,* chapters 8 through 10).

### Stay (Down)

The next step is to begin leaving your dog on Down-Stays via a signal (to command the Stay, not the Platz—we'll get to that part directly). Verbally order, "Platz," then cue Stay using the same signal for commanding Stay in the Sit position. The dog's knowledge of a signaled Sit-Stay spills over to the Down position, making this simple teaching. Distances and times should be increased at the same rate used with the Sit-Stay.

### Heeling

With your dog sitting at heel, having just completed some heeling under verbal command, gain attention through petting or similarly pleasant means. With your left arm at your side, flip your left hand forward and start walking. Though the odds that a dog might balk are slight, pat your left leg and repeat the signal if needed. Silently approve of your friend accompanying you by brief petting as you walk, assuming he's tall enough for you to reach him while walking. For a smaller dog, a smile and affirmative nods of your head will have to do, and they will be enough.

### Recall

The Recall signal is a quick, right-handed gesture toward your midsection. Leave the dog on a signaled Sit-Stay and step to leash's end. Signal the Recall and commence running backward, as you did when teaching the verbally commanded Recall. Praise silently by petting pooch's chin when he arrives and sits. A perfectly straight front-and-facing sit is presently of minor import—work on that aspect once the dog is doing well with the Recall signal. After three days, begin lessening your backward movement while increasing distance by a few feet daily.

## Finish

Verbally command the exercise two or three times in rapid succession using the spoken command. Then do so once using only the signal, which is little more than a hand flip to indicate direction: for the Inside Finish, signal with the left hand; for the Outside Finish, use the right. Initially accompany the cue with appropriate body language—turning your upper body toward the Finish direction—phasing out the mannerism as pooch learns.

## Stay (Standing)

Begin teaching the exercise by signaling Fuss. Stop after a few paces, and give and continue to hold the Stand signal: your right palm in front of the dog's eyes. If needed, lightly touch the outside flank with your left hand, or—if you're training a small canine—scoot your left foot underneath the animal's midsection, to freeze him in position. Return the signaling hand to your side. Before your pet can move, give the Stay hand signal. Move away a short distance for a few seconds. Increase this Stay's distance and duration over a few weeks until the working range is forty to fifty feet for as long as it takes you to walk that far, count to ten, and return.

## Down at a Distance

This signal's initial teaching stages constitute an exception to the rule of silent hand-signal instruction. To convey meaning properly, it's necessary to begin by using the spoken "Platz" timed with giving the hand signal.

First, verbally command, "Platz," to get your pal into a platzing frame of mind. Then leave him on a signal-commanded Sit-Stay and move to a point two or three feet in front of and facing him. Keep the leash in your left hand, with enough slack that the lead hangs just shy of the ground. As a quickly flowing sequence, raise your right palm—faced toward your dog—just above the level of your head. This is the Platz hand signal. Hold it there but a second, verbally command, "Platz," and

Teaching the Down at a Distance.

step with either foot onto the leash, letting the signaling hand fall to your side as you apply foot pressure. Generate adequate power to down your pet quickly, but make it suggestive, guiding pressure. Don't strike the lead with the same degree of force as you'd use in a refusal-to-comply correction. Foot-tap the lead. Your companion doesn't yet know what's going on because your altered command location makes this "new work" as far as he's concerned. Verbally praise, "Good Platz," once the dog is grounded, accenting the approval by repeating the hand signal. After a few seconds of praise, move the dog from the down position with, "C'mon, pup," or the like (as opposed to heeling the dog—we aren't working on heeling at present), and hurriedly repeat the exercise. Practice the sequence five or six times, then close the day's training.

When employing this guiding-foot-on-the-leash technique, move your foot no more than absolutely necessary when pinning the lead. Otherwise, pooch might learn a foot signal.

Once your dog has the idea, begin to soften and ultimately phase out the spoken "Platz." Increase by a few steps daily your distance when giving the signal.

### A Competition Note

Utility-Dog trainers using AKC format—consider the recommended Platz signal style: ". . . raise your right palm (faced toward the dog) just above the level of your head . . . hold it there but a second . . . [then let] the signaling hand fall to your side." An often-seen hand signal is a downward, sweeping motion. If that works for you, fine. My motives for using the signal described above are that it can be distinguished more easily at a distance, and that there's less chance that a judge might construe it to be two separate signals. That is, to make a downward motion, one first must raise the hand. Should the hand be raised and held in place for any length of time before bringing it down, a judge could rule that two signals had been given.

### Down from the Stand

Once your dog is doing well with the signaled Stand-Stay and the signaled Platz from the Sit, move on to signaling the Platz from the Stand. The method for teaching it is the same as teaching the signaled Platz from the Sit-Stay, described earlier.

Some dogs attempt to take a step or two when downing from the

The Platz hand signal.

The hand signal for Sit from the Down position.

Stand position. Overcome the problem by stepping toward (but *not* onto) the dog's front feet.

## Sit from Down

To teach this signal—an upward, sweeping, left-hand motion—first signal Platz from two or three feet. Once the animal is on *terra firma*, signal Sit and take a very quick, long step toward him. Your motion will likely induce the Sit, but temporarily add the verbal command to aid understanding. Praise, "Good Sit," as your pet rises. As he gets the idea, lessen your step-toward-the-dog movement until it disappears.

## Association Teaching

Another teaching method is to give a particular signal and immediately follow it with the corresponding verbal command, fading out the voice over time. Through this approach a dog learns that the signal means the trainer is about to speak the command, thus the animal performs through expectation. The technique is helpful should the direct approach fail, but it also can suggest an overall mind-set of anticipation, by which the dog is constantly trying to second-guess the trainer's next move. Left unchecked, such an attitude can grow into any number of problems.

## Reflection

Learning the value of silence is learning to listen to, instead of screaming at, reality: opening your mind enough to find what the end of someone's sentence sounds like, or listening to a dog until you discover what is needed instead of imposing yourself in the name of training.

Thomas Dobush, Monk of New Skete
(October 9, 1941–November 7, 1973)
*Gleanings*, the Journal of New Skete, Winter 1973

Freeze.

# 3

# The Guard Game

## "The *What?*"

Students often express that reaction when I introduce this topic. At my training seminars I habitually warm up by running my canine traveling companion through some obedience paces, having first set aside the animal's leash and collar. It's a relaxing way to collect myself, and my dogs are hams enough that the performance quickly captures crowd attention. Invariably someone asks, "How did you ever achieve such communication with your dog, such rapport? You're in new surroundings, around many strange dogs, your dog isn't even wearing a collar, yet it's obvious your control is absolute. How'd you do it?" My answer is always the same: "Sound training and the Guard Game." Then I start hearing, "The *what?*"—and the clinic is off and running.

## Characterized

The Guard Game is a fun technique for heightening attitude and reliability. Though the concept was suggested to me in 1977 by a German Shepherd Dog named Hawkeye, the Game hasn't had the circulation it might have had if I resided in a mainstream area.

Consider the following bird's-eye view of the Game itself. You're throwing pooch's beloved toy—let's say it's a tennis ball—for him to chase. After a return you take the object, set it on the ground, and command, "Guard." Having learned that he's not to touch a guarded object until it moves, your friend instantly rivets total concentration on the toy, placing his nose inches from it and freezing in place. You kick at the ball, deliberately missing it, the dog flinches in anticipation of the toy's flight. You boot at it several times in rapid succession, the dog follows each movement with jerks of his head. Suddenly your foot connects with the tennis ball and it bounds away with your teammate in hot pursuit. That's how the Guard Game is played. It teaches a dog that he's not to touch the designated object until he detects movement, and he is then to grab it as quickly as possible. The Game's effect on training is that it teaches a dog to concentrate for a prolonged period (initially on a toy, ultimately on the trainer), tuning out the world in the process.

## Compulsion Versus Drive

In general, training collars represent force, or pressure. Under my system the pinch collar is symbolic of this compulsion. For other trainers the choke collar serves the same purpose. A single object or concept correspondingly equable with drive is less easily identified. Frisbees, tennis balls and other toys generally serve more of a play function than as an aid to pure drive training. This is because play can be difficult to incorporate into obedience without loss of reliability.

The Guard Game fills that gap through the canine mind-set induced by the activity, and the spillover effect it has on a dog's perception of working. The Game is to drive as the collar is to compulsion. The activity sates a host of powerful drives: Prey, retrieve, play, dominance and—to an extent—fighting. The technique establishes rock-solid control that endures even when leash and collar aren't in use.

## Prerequisites

Prior to introducing the Game, the dog must be steadfast on Stays, and derive great pleasure in pursuit and apprehension of a play toy. For illustration purposes, I presume your primary play object is a tennis ball, though any similarly treasured, throwable article is equally effective.

## Commands

Three commands are taught with the Guard Game:
"Get It"    Pursue, bite and hold the play toy.

| "Guard" | Concentrate on the toy and Get It at the first sign of movement. |
|---|---|
| "Out" | Release the object and remain alert. |

## Preconditioning

For several weeks prior to the Game's formal introduction, command, "Get It," whenever you throw the ball for your pet. The purpose is to teach the command by linking its sound with the activity of pursuit and apprehension. If for some reason the animal doesn't chase the toy, don't push the issue. As the Game is drive-oriented, force has no place in its teaching. Refer to the section entitled "Foundational Training and the Playtoy" in Chapter 3 of *Dog Logic* for information about heightening interest in a play object.

## Testing Stay

Once the dog's attraction to the toy is very high—and not before—commence teaching the Game. Start a normal working session with some light, on-leash heeling. (Should your pet's work be markedly off, quit on a positive note and introduce the Game tomorrow.) Command, "Stay" (sitting), both verbally and with the hand signal (to avoid an obedience foul-up resulting from missed communication). Conduct the following test.

Holding the leash left-handed, use your right to bring the ball from a pocket. (Don't let pooch know beforehand that you have the toy with you.) Capture attention by waving the object in front of his muzzle. Once interest is evident, repeat the "Stay" command and drop the toy at a point two or three feet in front of the animal. (I seldom advocate giving a command twice, but in this instance it's warranted to avoid misunderstanding.) Your pal should continue to hold the Stay.

Maintain attention on him, as these actions can lead a dog to break position. Don't allow movement, but use only minimal pressure to keep your friend in the commanded position. Avoid putting a damper on this or any drive exercise. If the dog breaks, get him back in position while admonishing, "No—Stay," scoop up the ball, and restart the test. Continue until he holds the Stay as you drop the ball a short distance in front of him.

The purpose is to remind that, when you've commanded, "Stay," the position must be held irrespective of distractions. The first time your

Don't move as you throw the ball.

dog holds the Stay, despite the play toy being dropped in front of him, advance to teaching the Guard Game.

**Teaching the Guard Game**

Kneel next to your pet, to remove any towering, inhibiting image. Hold the ball inches from and slightly above your dog's nose. Suddenly switch your gaze to the object. Lend emphasis to the moment by quickly turning your head to accent your changed focal point, instead of merely shifting your eyes. This helps draw attention to the object. At the same instant, freeze your hand motion and command, "Guard," stretching the word in tones of anticipation and suspense. After only a second or two, before your friend can take any untoward action or become confused about what's expected, flip the play toy away without effecting any body movement that might distract. As you toss the object, encourage, "Get It, Get It." Praise, "Good Guard," as he gives pursuit, switching to "Good Get It" as he grabs the toy. Drop the leash as pooch departs, so not to risk an inadvertent correction as he bounds away—unintended pressure at this stage could have disastrous learning consequences. Call the dog back, marveling at what a Good Guard he performed. (True, Get It was the last thing he did but Guard is where we want to accent the praise at this time—he already knows the Get It phrase, but Guard is new material.) Allow a few seconds for your companion to feel proud of himself, then take the ball and repeat the lesson. Finally run through the sequence three more times, and end today's training.

**Procedures**

Two subtle technical aspects are involved here. First is always carrying the ball in a right-hand pocket. Ultimately this practice will draw your pet's attention during heeling more toward you—across your body— not just to the ball, than if you were to stow it in a nearer-to-him, left-side pocket. Second, when producing the object and commanding, "Guard," the technique of holding the toy immediately in front of and slightly above the dog's nose is to keep him positioned. If the ball is held significantly above or, far from the animal, he'd be more likely to jump up or forward than to operate from a posture of your control. Were the toy held below the muzzle, the dog might tune you out—the ball's location could block the animal's focus. He might be more difficult to control, and you'd be unable to read him as easily.

**Freeze**

Avoid making even slight hand motions after commanding, "Guard." We're teaching your friend to key on the object's movement, not yours. Don't give the command and then fake-flick your wrist or pull your arm back for a long toss. Post-command movement could risk not only confusion and a premature response, but your hand being nipped as well.


## THE RELEASE

### "Out!"

Many a dog comes to enjoy the Guard Game so much that he drops the ball upon returning to the handler, effectively asking too play the Game again. Whether to teach the Out ("Release It!") command now depends on your canine's temperamental toughness and jaw strength.

With a soft-mouthed animal the command can be instigated through association: withdrawing the toy, timed with the Out cue. Later it may be necessary to reinforce through compulsion (as described below), but that aspect should be delayed until your pet's drive for the Game is sufficiently high that force won't dampen enthusiasm.

However, if your dog has jaws like a bench vise, don't use the association technique, for three reasons. First, for all a dog could presently know of Out's meaning, he might think you're saying, "Let's play tug-of-war." Second, even if the animal were to comprehend Out's message of Release, should his jaw pressure be such that you can't wrest the toy from him, you'd be demonstrating that Out allows for optional compliance, essentially saying, "Resist me if you can." Third, were compulsion needed to cause the object's release, its use during the instructive phases could lessen interest in and understanding of the Game.

"So if my dog is of the *Jaws* persuasion, how do I get the toy from him?"

Try *replacement*. Drop a food bit or a second toy and see what happens. Or use minimal force: a tap *under* the jaw (*under*, to prevent head-shyness—pooch won't see the hand coming). Or grab the play object and lift—bringing the dog's front end off the ground if need be—pulling the toy toward either side of the mouth. Or reach across the muzzle and hook a finger behind a canine (longest upper) tooth. This technique usually causes any dog to open up, but it can be risky in terms of being bitten if the hand is not quickly withdrawn. Once control of the play toy is secured, immediately command, "Guard," and fire up the Game. The dog will learn to release to be able to chase the object again.

### Drive Basis of the Out Command

From a motivational perspective, Out is better rooted in drive than compulsion. A message of "Release the toy and remain alert to play the Game again" is preferable to "Let go to avoid pressure." Still, the drive approach isn't always possible, as some animals can respect only force once they're keyed on a pursuit object. The category your friend falls under hinges upon your reading of his intensity level. If yours is a suggestible animal, you'll accomplish more by communicating he should release the article to be ready to chase it again. This may make little sense in human terms, but it speaks volumes to a dog. The human reaction is that no purpose is served by dropping an object only to have to pursue it again, but a canine often enjoys the chase as much or more than he does simple possession.

### Compulsion Basis of the Out Command

Should your pet refuse to surrender the toy, apply pressure in one of two ways. Choose the method suitable to your animal's size, toughness, and determination.

With a dog of softer temperament, first direct, "Sit." Praise, "Good Sit," and let a few seconds pass, so the upcoming force won't be misconstrued with the act of sitting on command. Standing at the animal's right side, command, "Out." Allow a second or two for compliance—your friend may need that long to disengage the object. If it's apparent he has no intention of releasing, exert steadily increasing, leash/pinch-collar pressure, upward and slightly toward your right (assuming pooch is in the Heel position), until he drops the toy. (Don't use this technique if you're using a choke: the purpose is not to hang the dog. For the same reason, don't use this method with a small animal—the idea isn't to take him off the ground.) Don't jerk the leash—pull it. The ball will drop when the dog yips in response to the force.

With a tougher, less touch-sensitive dog, or with one whose body mass is so slight that leash pressure would lift him, grasp (*don't* use your fingernails) the flank farthest from you and apply enough squeezing compression to cause dropping the toy. Light finger pressure usually does the job. As before, the toy will fall away as the dog opens his mouth. When using this technique, despite the severity with which it's applied,

The flank method of teaching the Out.

One purpose of the Guard Game is to teach a dog to concentrate.

a dog will often reflexively spin toward the source of the pressure. Don't wait for your eyes to tell you he's moving—by then your hand may need stitches. Squeeze the flank and remove your hand, all in the same motion.

*As* the animal releases the object—whether in response to collar or flank pressure—praise, "Good Out," and in the same breath, command, "Guard," then *immediately* kick the toy away while encouraging pooch to "Get It." Once he drops the object, you should have him chasing it within two seconds. Again, we're trying to say that it's in his interests to drop the article so you can make it run away for him to chase.

## Canine Focus and Handler Safety

Two common denominators present in the foregoing compulsion techniques deal with pressure and anger. Collar or flank pressure causes release of an object: the dog gasps in response to force, and a by-product is the ball falling from his mouth. The article is then kicked away forthwith to reward the animal for dropping the ball. The quick kick is also to provide a focal outlet for any anger the dog might feel from the pressure or over the loss of the play toy. With a very tough, high-fired canine, the purpose of the quick kick can be to keep him off you.

## Testing

After a few days, conduct two tests to see if your student is comprehending the Game. First, with your pal in a Sit-Stay, place yourself at an angle to his right so you can read his facial features. Keep the leash in your left hand to prevent lunging. Using your right hand, hold the ball above and in front of him, a foot or two from the muzzle. Command, "Guard." A second or two later, *barely* flick your hand. The movement should be almost imperceptible. Watch your dog's eyes—his eyelids should flutter in response to the hand movement. If they do, he's obviously getting the message. If they don't, he needs more time to assimilate the Game's objective. Either way, quickly complete the Game by throwing the ball, praising as he gives chase.

The second test can immediately follow the first. Sit-Stay your pet, hold the ball as before, and command, "Guard." With no more finger movement than is needed, release the toy. Don't toss it—just allow gravity to pull it from your hand. The dog should be pouncing toward the object before or as it lands. This test confirms that your pal is keying not on hand motion but on the tennis ball's movement. If you read that pooch is keying on your movement instead of the toy's, work at greatly decreasing your motion when throwing the ball.

## Progression

A variation on the Game is teaching that the toy should be guarded even though it's been placed on the ground. Command "Platz," add "Stay" for clarity of intent, and set the ball on the ground a few inches in front of your charge. Command "Guard." If he looks up at you questioningly (since the object isn't in your hand, as it's been before), make a light foot-tap atop the ball and repeat, "Guard." Kick slightly at the play toy once without touching it, wait a beat, then boot the object away, encouraging pursuit. Should your pet try to grab the ball in response to the foot movement, tell him, "No—Guard," make one more foot fake, then kick the toy away. (When kicking at the toy, keep the distance your foot travels to a minimum. Otherwise the dog can learn to watch your foot instead of the play toy.) Over time, increase the number of foot feints before booting the toy.

Another variation can be started once "Guard" causes your dog to focus exclusively on the toy. Place the ball on the ground, and command, "Guard," without first telling the animal, "Platz." As he stands and rivets attention on the object, *gently* walk into his side, causing him to move out of your way. Do this in a lightly brushing manner—don't harshly bump the dog. The idea isn't to distract him—it's to cause him to move slightly while maintaining attention on the toy. Should he look toward you in response to being touched, command, "Guard," a second time, tapping the ball with your toe to refocus attention. As he resumes a Pointer-like stance, lightly bump him again, then kick the ball away. In time you'll be able to cause your dog to move in a full 360-degree arc around the play toy while keeping his attention riveted on it.

What's taking place is extension of two *Dog Logic* reinforcement concepts: The *Resistance Stay* technique, outlined in chapter 9, and the *challenge heeling* concept, described in chapter 10. You're causing your friend to work harder by making his "job" a bit more difficult, the purpose being to intensify his sense of accomplishment.

## Equipment Change

As soon as you can dispense with a leash—the barometer of your pet's reliability to the Game's Stay element—replace its often-in-the-way length with a *collar tab*. The tab is a short length of venetian-blind cord, or similar material, tied to the collar's live ring. Its purpose is to provide a quick handle. This change marks a subtle first step toward off-leash work.

### Distance

Once your companion has mastered the foregoing elements of the Guard Game, adapt the lessons to distance work. Start by commanding, "Sit—Stay." Move to a point three feet in front of the dog, produce the ball, and command, "Guard." A second or so later, hurl the toy away, urging, "Get It."

Play the Game five or six times, gradually lengthening distance from your pet before commanding, "Guard." By session's end you should be operating at five to ten feet. Of course, don't go to five feet until pooch is Stay-steady at four; don't move to six feet until he's solid at five, and so on. A week or ten days should find you at twenty to forty feet, depending how your dog adjusts.

### I've Been Asked . . .

By itself, the Guard Game does not produce a guard dog. It can aid in establishing a foundation for such training, should that be your goal, but the Game itself should not turn your dog into an aggressive threat.

## APPLICATIONS

### With Heeling

After a few minutes of on-leash heeling, whip the ball from your pocket as you stop. Hold it in front of your dog's "beak" and command, "Guard." (The animal may Sit at this cessation of motion, but more likely he'll freeze in a standing or half-sitting position. Don't correct him should he not Auto-Sit; "Guard" overrides all commands, including the nonverbalized Automatic Sit.) Wait a second or two, then throw the toy and cheer on your pet, "Get It." Afterward, note how this single application has heightened your pal's concentration on you during heeling. Why? Because he's hoping you'll play the Game again. Later, through habit formation, he'll focus on you for longer periods during heeling.

## With Platz

With your dog sitting at heel, command, "Platz." *As he touches the ground*—timing is crucial here—immediately produce the previously concealed ball, hold it inches in front of his muzzle and command, "Guard." Let only a second or two lapse before tossing the toy, encouraging, "Get It." Repeat the sequence three times and remain at this stage for three days before progressing.

During the next phase, command, "Platz," and—after the animal has been grounded for a few seconds—heel him away without playing the Game. Stop after a few steps. After the Auto-Sit, again command, "Platz." This time start the Game the instant pooch lies down. What we're doing is making the Game a random occurrence, rather than a constant one. The Guard Game *may* be played after Platz, but *When?* can't be predicted. The idea is to speed up your pet's reaction of hitting the ground—which he'll do to play the Game—and to heighten attitude toward the Platz command.

If at any time the dog fails to down when commanded, immediately revert to compulsion and suspend the Game for a few days. Once the animal's response to the command is satisfactory again, bring the Game back into the sessions randomly.

## With Stays

Leave your friend on a Sit-Stay. While walking away, suddenly turn and underhand the ball toward him, commanding, "Get It," as he give chase. While this isn't a Guard Game application *per se*, the Game does heighten attraction to the toy, and once a dog learns that you'll sometimes throw the ball to him during a Stay, he'll build the habit of focusing on you while you're away.

## With Recalls

During a working session, command, "Stay," and go a significant distance—thirty feet or so. Then Recall pooch, "Here." The instant he arrives and sits, produce the ball—which he didn't know you had with you—freeze it is front of his nose, and command, "Guard." After a second or two, flip it away, prompting, "Get It." After the animal dashes back to you with his prize, take the toy and repeat the exercise. This time, with the dog remembering he got to play the Game when he last came to you, he Recalls as though his tail were on fire. Speedy Recalls are being established as a habit, as is heightened attention on you upon arrival.

The next day, start a session by calling your dog, *without him being aware you have the tennis ball.* As he arrives, produce the toy, command, "Guard," and quickly make the toss, commanding, "Get It." Praise him lavishly when he returns and end the session. Do no more work just then. Hours later, open a working period by leaving the animal on a Stay, then calling, "Here." He'll respond with blazing speed. Don't play the Game this time, though. Praise "Good Here," command, "Stay," leave quickly and call him again from several yards distant. As he arrives and sits, bring out the toy, command, "Guard," and complete the Game. This makes the Game a more random event, and further instills the mind-set of a furiously quick Recall. The dog learns that—while he may not get to play the Game every time—it's in his interests to respond quickly because you *might* fire up the Game. Long-term he develops the habit of coming quickly because it's the only way he knows.

**With the Finish**

During another training session, play the Guard Game just after a Finish. You'll soon observe a much faster and flashier reaction to the Finish command. Once you see this heightened response, play the Game after heeling your pet a few steps from the Finish position, instead of immediately after he executes it. The idea is to place the potential for the Game later in the sequence, to accent the "When?" element.

**Attention**

Prior to today's session, pass an easily breakable thread through the ball, tying it so it can be necklaced a few inches below your chin. Zip a jacket to within inches below the tennis ball, so the toy is visible. Tomorrow, fasten the garment a couple of inches higher. Close it higher still the day after that, and so on, until the ball can no longer be seen.

Throughout this procedure, snap the object from your neck whenever the spirit moves you, command, "Guard," and let the toy fly. Pooch will learn that the ball is always located at a point inches below your chin. Note the effect during Heeling and Recalls in terms of where and to what degree he fixes attention on you.

## Instant On

Two added pluses of the Game are the increased attraction a dog will have toward the play toy, and the uses to which one can put this heightened interest. An obvious application is teaching a canine to react instantly to his name. I know, your dog knows his name. But does he reflexively turn toward you when you say it, even when he's in a sound sleep, or when he's in playful pursuit of another object or animal? Try the following.

While throwing the play toy (but not while playing the Guard Game), bring your arm back for a long toss. As the animal darts away in anticipation of pursuit, speak his name crisply. When he stops his flight and looks back toward you—and that may take a few seconds; he looks frantically for the ball first—gently toss the object underhanded toward his mouth. Then praise with "Good [Name]" as he attempts to grab the toy, regardless whether he catches it. After a few subsequent long throws, do the fake-out, long-toss again, following it by saying the dog's name and throwing the play toy to him *as he turns* toward you. A day or two later, modify the pattern to hurling the toy (underhanded and gently, always) *as* you say his name. You'll soon find your friend's attention is instantaneous when hearing his name. Most dogs enjoy a sudden and immediate challenge to apprehend a prey/play object. That's why and how this technique works. The dog learns that upon hearing his name, he has but an instant to turn toward its sound, or he won't be able to snatch the toy out of the air.

To conclude this lesson, after a few weeks of the foregoing training, speak your dog's name. As he turns toward you he may freeze in place, anticipating the toy's flight in his direction. If he does, call him to you, not with the formal Recall command, "Here," but on the order of, "C'mere, pup." *As your pet takes his first step* toward you, toss ball to him. The next time you call the animal, let him take two or three steps before you flip the toy his way. What's left is allowing your companion to take a few more steps each time you call him. The result is a dog who comes reliably and quickly in response to the sound of his name.

## Applications Summary

These are but a few of many applications that can be made of the Guard Game. Beyond its enjoyment value for dog and handler, the Game's primary training purpose is to teach concentration on one behavior for prolonged periods. Secondary functions are laying foundations for

40

retrieving and/or protection work by heightening prey and play drives. Tertiary benefits include enhanced animation and increased fixation on the trainer. Lest one begin to view the Game in working contexts only, remember it's a Game first, and its main use is during playtime.

The Game's central working employment is to heighten enjoyment of activities with which it is associated. It's to make the particular exercise—Platz, Heeling, Recall, Sit, Stay or whatever—more fun for your dog without risking loss of reliability. The key is random usage. If the animal learns that you'll always (or never) play the Game, its effectiveness quickly deteriorates. If he realizes that the two of you will share the Game at unpredictable times, your pet will stay up emotionally in anticipation of playing the Guard Game. In time this upbeat mind-set will be your pet's working attitude, for reasons he won't even remember. It will simply be part of him.

**Reflection**

> *The yellowest cur I ever knew*
> *Was to the boy who loved him true.*
> Unknown, *The Dog*

# 4

# Off-Leash/Off-Collar Obedience

---

## Overview

Most initial phases of off-leash/off-collar work are best presented to pooch as something of a bluff.

By now your student has doubtless observed that you possess powers and capabilities he can't fully comprehend. You can make a play toy fly over great distances. A movement of your hand illuminates a room as you enter, darkens it as you leave. You know what your companion is doing even when you aren't present, such as during Out-Of-Sight Stays. Your dog learns to accept such phenomena without grasping how they occur. Similarly, he learns that you have inexplicable abilities to contact him physically across wide distances, to govern his actions without appearing to have the means to do so. That's what I mean about running a bluff.

The rationale behind this approach is it addresses real-world situations. Consider: If one is several hundred feet from his or her pet, there's no way the dog can be physically forced to do (or not do) anything, short of using a shock collar. The trick is not to let pooch discover this fact.

Rapport ultimately supplants mechanical and procedural techniques. Various training methods are necessary toward finalizing the process, however. A dog will always be a dog (thank God), and until the animal realizes you are pack leader and are totally in control (despite occasional appearances to the contrary), the human-canine relationship cannot develop to its full potential.

Now, before getting this chapter's lessons underway, we must examine a related matter.

### Something to Think About

I bet we've something in common, you and I: neither of us condones canine mistreatment. Whether the specifics relate to substandard care or out-and-out abuse, we deplore it.

When pondered in an obedience context, the preceding may conjure images of abuse through overcorrection. It's a loathsome practice, one that's sadly all too common. Some methods foisted in the name of training are sufficient to turn one's stomach, sometimes generating an urge to break a few laws in a hapless animal's defense.

A related, yet less acknowledged, brand of cruelty is undercorrection. While practitioners may believe they're motivated by kindness, the habit is but another extreme, representing comparable mistreatment.

In theory, whether working on- or off-leash, suited-to-the-dog corrections should be made with the same degree of force, no more, no less. In practice, though, trainers sometimes slip into the trap of nagging-type corrections. This usually occurs during the on-lead phase.

The critter Sits very slowly or markedly crooked:
*"Well, at least he sat."*

It takes three progressively louder Platz commands to get the dog onto the ground:
*"Should I have corrected after my first command?"*

Attention during heeling is everywhere but on the handler:
*"I'll just give a leash flick here. No sense in getting after pooch."*

In all three instances, and others like them, lack of appropriate correction guarantees the problem will continue. It delays an inevitable confrontation, ultimately leading to more force than was originally needed. The dog learns—moreover he is taught—he can "get away with it."

This tendency toward undercorrection arises chiefly where—prior to obedience training—the dog was nearly uncontrollable. Undesirable behaviors decrease after a few lessons, and the owner is so gratified that he doesn't follow through when the situation calls for it. He compares current deportment against what it was, not against what it could be. He begins to back away from the level of pressure that has brought the two of them this far, and what the dog's obedience might have been never comes to pass. In some cases, behavior backslides. Pooch comes to perceive the reduced force as a periodic annoyance instead of an avoidable consequence.

Failing a change in trainer attitude, punishment will always be part of the dog's life. Seldom will a day be free of pressure. Though it's true the corrections are never very firm, it's equally true they'll never stop. In a very real sense, the result is a canine serving a life sentence of abuse.

One can get by with repetitious, minor corrections with an on-leash dog. But a similar approach to off-leash training cannot and will not produce reliability. For example, should be trainer be using a light line (a long, thin line) in place of a leash, and should he repeatedly undercorrect to the extent that the animal learns that the line is nothing more than a long, thin leash, then all the trainer has done is swap equipment. In essence, the dog is still on-leash.

That corrections must always be slightly tougher than the canine in question is even truer during off-leash work because they can't be repeated *ad infinitum*. Once the animal is truly off-lead, no physical means exist to effect behavior. Correction and praise must have accomplished their purpose by then.

Must a trainer be tougher during off-lead work than a dog's capacity to absorb correction? No. Of course not. That's never right. Though if you've slid into the undercorrection trap, stay on-lead awhile and realign compulsion with your pet's sensitivity before proceeding. Otherwise you'll be framing off-lead control atop a weak, shaky foundation. Then the outcome isn't just predictable, it's inevitable: the training will come apart, most likely in a situation where obedience is really needed.


## EQUIPMENT

### Basic Tools, Revisited

Off-leash obedience is taught through much the same training mechanics as the on-lead program. Drive and compulsion are still the keys. Other than the bluff concept, the primary instructional difference is the use of additional equipment during off-lead work.

45

Attaching a piece of brightly-tinted yarn facilitates locating a throw chain in tall grass or snow.

A collar tab.

46

**Throw Chain**

Owners are sometimes shocked when first hearing about the *throw-chain* concept.

"Let me get this straight: you actually throw a length of chain at your dog? At man's best friend?"

Answer: Yes, but be aware that we're not discussing heavyweight material here, but bare ounces of hanging-lamp chain.* A trainer throws it at his off-leash dog should the animal depart despite the pack leader's expressed wishes to the contrary. The goal is hardly to hurt or injure pooch—far from it. It's to startle, and to give him pause as to how the trainer did that: touched him at a distance. This is why I tell students:

> Don't try for maximum throwing velocity. Remember, pain is *not* the purpose here. We're after the "Gotcha!" effect. Besides, the harder the throw the greater the likelihood of missing, which could frustrate you and perhaps amuse the dog.

The chain should be hurled only when the animal is turned away, so not to risk striking an eye or revealing your ace. Also, you must be adept at hitting a moving object and able to read that the dog is about to break, to react in time to throw the chain accurately at an accelerating canine's receding hindquarters. Waiting until your dog is in full stride will have him out of range before you can hurl the projectile. Effective usage has the chain striking pooch before he's taken three bounds.

Once your charge is back in line, don't retrieve the chain. Should he observe you reclaiming it, he could figure out (in his own way) what transpired, which would greatly lessen the tool's effectiveness. Carry several chains, later picking up spent ones after taking your pet from the area.

**Collar Tab**

A collar tab is an appropriate length of venetian-blind cord or similar material. Looped through the collar's live ring, it provides a quick handle. A tab shouldn't be so long that the dog might catch a paw in the loop. With small dogs a loop needn't be made—a single line of cord is sufficient. Like the collar, the tab should never be left on an unattended animal.

The tab is often used in concert with a throw chain. Let's say your

---

*Attaching a piece of brightly tinted yarn facilitates locating the object in tall grass or snow.

off-leash student bolts during heeling. You accurately hurl the chain at his *derrière,* verbal-bridging, "No!" just as it strikes, and seconds later collar-correct the animal via the tab, reminding him, "Fuss!" The throw chain halts his flight; the collar tab provides a quick handle for reestablishing control.

### Light Line

A light line is a long, thin, lightweight cord with as light a snap as will hold the dog. I've used lengths varying from fifteen to one hundred feet. Material can range from venetian-blind cord to fishing line, depending on the animal's size and strength. A hand loop is neither necessary nor desirable. The line should be able to be dragged safely, without a loop that could catch on brush and the like. Gloves may be necessary to avoid cuts and friction burns from the line. Usage of this equipment follows under "Applications and Techniques."

### Light Lead

A light lead is a six-foot leash appreciably lighter in weight than the primary lead. If you've been using a leather leash, a show lead will do. If a show lead is your primary leash, fishing line is adequate. Light-lead usage follows under "Applications and Techniques."

## APPLICATIONS AND TECHNIQUES

### Multiple Leashing

Initiate a working session with some brief, on-leash heeling. Following an Automatic Sit, praise while sneaking a light leash onto your pet's collar (don't remove the primary leash, though). Keep pooch unaware of the second lead's presence. While holding both leashes in either hand, heel a few more steps. Stop, remove the primary lead, and hurl it a few feet in front of and slightly to your dog's left, radiating smug disdain for the object: "We don't need *this* any longer, do we, pup!" Draw your companion's attention to the illusion that he's free of any restraint, concealing the second lead's excess right-handed behind your back. Command, "Fuss," and step off confidently.

One of three situations will develop: Your pet will heel along with you; or, he'll remain in place; or, he'll toddle off in pursuit of other activities.

48

Should your dog trot with you as commanded, fine. Many adapt to off-leash routines without contention, having gotten such arguments out of their systems during on-lead work. Praise, "Good Fuss," and, after a few moments, return to the discarded primary leash. Make a show of fastening it, accenting that it's been among the missing. Leave the second leash connected, carrying both with either hand. Heel briefly, repeat the full sequence once, and end today's work. The training now entails more of the foregoing over longer periods of time, and in the face of ever-increasing distractions.

If your dog is like some I've known, once he senses he's shed of constraint, he'll remain in place or be gone for the tall timber, more often the latter. Should the dog remain stationary, a tug on the secondary lead timed with a second "Fuss" is adequate correction. Should the animal attempt to flee, it's time to clarify a few things.

Allowing for size and temperament, the correction must fit the crime. Remember, the nature of double-leash training is such that one can't rely on days of minor corrections to do the job. Should your pet figure out that all you've done is switch leads, then that's all you've done: change leashes. The idea to convey is, "Don't push me, dog. Don't abuse my trust in you."

Just after the animal hits the end of the lead, chastise, "No!" As he turns in your direction, indicating that he's not going to rebel further, let the lead slip from your hands, dropping it such that you can reclaim it in a blink should the need arise. Keep your hands at your sides as and after you drop the leash, effecting an open-palms posture that displays you're holding air. This seeming lack of means won't be lost on the dog. Go to him, walking along the lead in case the student again tests the teacher's influence. Point out, "I said, 'Fuss,' " covertly palm the light lead, and heel to the primary leash. Assuming the animal doesn't push the issue further today (most won't), methodically and with obvious purpose attach the main leash. Command, "Sit" (to finish on a high note), praise, "Good Sit," and pet your pal to show you feel no anger. Then take him from the area. Don't train further today.

Consider the events of the past few minutes. Should pooch run off once you've removed the primary lead, it's better to end the session soon after enforcing your will. If the workout isn't terminated shortly thereafter—moreover, if the series is repeated—the animal has an opportunity to evaluate specifically what transpired when he thought he was freed from control.

The memory with which to leave the dog is this: You removed the leash, he tried to exploit the situation and the roof inexplicably fell in.

Something went very wrong at a time when he was certain you couldn't affect his actions. "Wha' hoppened? My leader removed the leash, but when I ran away, he somehow controlled me."

During the next training period, concentrate on any obedience aspects *other than* off-leash work. Let today's lesson simmer for a while. Then repeat the double-leash sequence. Be aware the dog may pay more attention to what's going on than previously. Thus, be extra sneaky when attaching the secondary lead. Don't tip your hand.

When ending a training session, remove the backup leash while attaching the primary one. Otherwise your pal may notice the second lead's presence. Once it's detached from the collar, drop the extra lead where you're standing and heel away quickly, lest pooch notice it. Reclaim the second leash after taking your worker from the area.

A few successful outings don't prove reliability. If at some point the animal is going to flee the scene, better he do so in a controlled setting conducive to teaching. Understand: The purpose behind such technique is to create situations such that—if your pet is ultimately going to take off—you're in a position to affirm that obedience must be absolute, despite apparent presence or absence of a leash.

### A Pointless Tactic

Students sometimes tell me, "Last week I sneaked the leash off my dog's collar for a while, and he heeled just fine."

Sure. "That's because only one of you knew the animal was off-leash."

When advancing to multiple-leash techniques, make no secret that the primary leash has been removed. You want pooch to know it's gone. Otherwise, you can't predict how he'll respond once the lead is truly off.

### The Recall Subterfuge

A favored ruse for establishing off-leash control ostensibly relates to the Recall exercise. The technique should be applied only once during a three- to four-week period. Otherwise a dog could learn too much. Like the preceding multiple-leash lesson, an auxiliary concept is preventing a canine from discovering the exercise's nuts-and-bolts. The idea is still to leave him with the impression that even though appearances suggested he wasn't under your domination, he was.

Before bringing your best friend to the training site, extend a twenty- to fifty-foot light line across the area. Then go get pooch and do some on-leash heeling (to establish control, and to warm up your pal). Next, heel to one end of the line. After the Auto-Sit, while praising and petting, surreptitiously attach line to collar. Remove the leash, make sure your pet sees you toss it aside, command "Stay," and proceed to the line's other end. Once there, drop your hat or some such so you've an obvious reason to bend over—dogs may be dumb animals but they're not stupid. As you retrieve the fallen article, covertly grip the line. Give a *light* tug, and immediately call your pet: "Here."

No, those last two instructions aren't backward. Normally you'd pull on the line *just after* giving the command. Today, however, you'll seemingly make a technical error: pulling the line *just before* commanding, "Here." The purpose isn't to effect a correction (hence, the stipulated "*light* tug")—it's to contact the dog when he thought you couldn't. Properly done, the animal will feel the resultant minor pressure an instant before or as he hears you call.

What's taking place isn't a Recall exercise at all. It only looks that way. What's actually being said to your charge is *you can touch him at a distance*. As he arrives and sits, stealthily remove the line and drop it while praising and petting. Leave the line where it falls, instead of calling attention to it by picking it up. Take pooch from the training area for some quiet, solitary contemplation of what's just occurred. Further work at this point could obscure the lesson.

### "How'd He Do That?"

Off-lead control can be enhanced by even more subtle, less-direct methods.* Allow your dog to drag a light line while the two of you are playing ball. After a few minutes, call him to you, *not* in the context of a formal Recall, but more on the order of, "C'mere, pup." Should the animal run past or away from you, keep your hands at your sides while stepping on the line. The intent isn't to apply a forceful correction, bringing the critter to an abrupt, bone-jarring halt. It's to slow and impede flight. When the dog looks back—and sees nothing in your hands—he'll wonder for a month how you controlled him.

What's sought here is the *spillover effect*, whereby the gist of a seemingly nonstructured event seeps into all areas of reliability. That's why the lesson is best not conducted in a training setting, *per se*. You

---

*Don't use this technique until your dog's drive for the play toy is strong, lest any pressure diminish attraction to it.

and your friend were playing, he wasn't in a working mind-set, and suddenly your apparently nonexistent control was in effect. This is a powerful lesson, especially in its long-range implications.

## A Not-So-Obvious Plus

An added benefit of the foregoing technique is its effect in making a dog more reliable in coming to you in other than formal Recall settings. It's one matter for him to respond with patterned behavior when he's been left on a Stay. Then he's under your domination from the moment you leave him. But when the animal is running free, and he perhaps spots a rabbit or some such to chase, conventional Recall training may fall short. The reason is that in this instance you're attempting to establish control when your pet—not you—is in charge.

## Spillover Consequences

As suggested earlier, the preceding light-line procedures can have quite a carryover effect into other aspects of your friend's obedience. All phases of a dog's work often improve soon after starting off-leash training. The animal learns you can physically control him at your whim without appearing to be able to do so. What pooch won't figure out is how. He may discover the light line, and that your power has something to do with it, but he has no way of knowing just how long the cord is, or into what areas of his life it can reach. For all the animal knows, it may be of infinite length and unlimited potential. Eventually he accepts the condition without understanding the whys and the wherefores. To underscore this chapter's opening statement, that's what's meant about initial off-leash work being something of a bluff.

## Through the Back Door

Another technique is throwing the play toy and, once your pal has grabbed it, if the animal is returning, take a step or two backward (to heighten attraction) and informally say, ''C'mere, pup,'' while patting your leg. Sure, it was his idea to return, but make him think it was yours. Later, all the dog will remember is coming while hearing your call.

Using hands to Sit a dog bereft of collar.

## Clarification

If all this strikes you as "training by confusion," you're right. If such technique seems flawed by definition, or immoral, unethical, or less than forthright, you're missing the point.

That a confused dog shouldn't be corrected is maintained throughout my training books. But if you command your off-leash pet to "Fuss," and he responds by lighting out for the hinterlands, the animal is hardly confused—he knows exactly what he's doing. He determined you had no physical control of him, and he decided to take advantage of the situation. That bespeaks a calculating canine, not a confused one.

Because such behavior is intolerable, you must be equipped to respond in a way that says, "It's in your best interests not to try that again." You can't outrun pooch, you lack his ability for quick starts and sudden turns, but when it comes to being downright sneaky, he's met his match: you can surely out-think him. As stated in *Dog Logic*'s fifth chapter, "Training Guidelines," ". . . be one inch tougher than the dog, no more, no less." Toughness relative to *Canis familiaris* is an attribute of varying qualities. It's not limited to physical force. Mental toughness is part of the equation, too.

## A Quick Hitter

Another off-leash reinforcer can occur in and around the house. For example, you encounter your dog and say in passing, "Howdy, pup—Sit." Praise the animal if he complies; immediately cause him to sit if he doesn't. Compulsion can be effected by using your hands like a pinch collar—pulling the skin on the neck upward and toward yourself, similar to how you taught the on-leash Sit. Don't dig in with your nails—use your fingertips. The idea is to control, not to frighten or injure.

After the dog obeys, pet him and say, "Good Sit, pup. See you later," and depart. If "later" is your release cue, the phrase allows the animal to leave the Sit. If a release cue isn't part of your training plan, bring the dog out of the Sit by patting your leg, scratching his ears, commenting, "You're sure a neat dog," and going about your business.

The entire "training session" lasted only seconds, but much was accomplished. Obedience was activated in a blink, and *no collar was required for control*. Only your presence was needed. The nature of such subtle conditioning builds lifelong habits.

## OFF-COLLAR OBEDIENCE

### In General

The final objective is to work your companion totally without collar. If he is never brought to that point of reliability, obedience will always be contingent upon equipment rather than thoroughness of training. Once the dog is operating at this ultimate level, use a choker or a leather or cloth collar for trips to town at any situations requiring a collar's use.

Rapport eventually replaces mechanical off-leash and off-collar training. Despite distractions, were any of my dogs to break from me (except to protect me or mine), I might topple into a dead faint. They've been through this chapter's off-lead techniques, but more important is the influence of unity between us. This bonding level is a direct offshoot of pack instinct operating in conjunction with effective training.

### Off-Collar Training

To establish off-collar control systematically, first bring your pet to a point of unshakable off-leash reliability. Off-collar obedience then becomes an easily-achieved objective.

Train at first in a comparatively small, securely fenced, distraction-free area. Carry a pocketful of compulsion and an equal amount of drive: throw chains and a tennis ball.

Teaching periods should be less structured than those preceding. Since off-collar obedience is intended for immediate, *ad hoc* use, it's better taught in an atmosphere of spontaneity. By advancing to this level of communication, you bring obedience to the real world (which can be pretty unstructured).

Begin with a few minutes of off-leash work: Heeling, Recalls, or whatever you like. Then remove the collar, toss it aside (making certain pooch notices its passing), and continue as though nothing unusual had happened.

Should your pet react by breaking headlong away, off-collar work is obviously premature. More foundational on- and off-leash training is needed. Assuming the animal remained at your side, make your first command "Sit" or "Platz." (It's better to initiate off-collar training with a static command than with a moving one. Doing so raises the odds of achieving first-time success. To start with Heeling, for instance, could lead a dog to break as he'd already be in motion.) As your companion complies, praise "Good Sit" (or "Good Platz"), and immediately command "Fuss." Move out briskly, but go only four or five paces. When you stop, do so abruptly. This distinct go-and-stop style can capture a canine's deepest attention (as can dead-slow heeling interspersed with brief sprints). As he Auto-Sits, impart sincere, calm praise. While you're at it, pat yourself on the back, too. You've obviously accomplished a great deal.

Next, initiate a few run-throughs of the Guard Game (if you've not taught the Game, just throw the play toy for pooch). After a few minutes, and at a time when he's carrying the toy and is fairly close to you, command, "Out" (assuming your friend knows the command—skip this part if he doesn't). If need be, rapidly repeat the command several times while quickly moving toward him. *Just as* he drops the ball, praise, "Good Out," and immediately boot the toy away, commanding, "Get It." After your pal returns, attach leash and collar, love him up a bit, and end the period.

Three reasons underlie ending the session with the Guard Game (or merely throwing the toy), interrupted with "Out" followed by "Get It." First, the workout terminates on as high a note as could be asked: your companion pursuing his beloved play toy. Second, by causing the animal to suddenly drop the object, your command is overriding very strong drives and equally pronounced learned behaviors, thereby accenting your pack-leader status. Last, you're combining work and play to the extent that they will ultimately merge into one concept in your dog's mind: obedience. The task now becomes similar training, and gradually adding distractions as the two of you progress.

### Reflection

The censure of a dog is something no man can stand.
Christopher Morley, *The Haunted Bookshop*

# 5

# Motion Exercises

---

## Characterized

Motion obedience requires a moving dog to respond to a static command: "Sit," "Platz" or "Wait." Commands are given at a distance or during heeling, and those during heeling are given without the handler coming to a stop.

Motion training is eminently functional as obedience is sometimes needed hurriedly. There isn't always time to go through a rigid sequence to achieve a desired end. For example, until now when you've needed your dog to Platz during heeling, you first had to stop, wait for the animal to Sit, then command, "Platz" (and some handlers add, "Stay"), before you could leave. In motion training, the dog learns to immediately assume and hold a position in response to a single command, regardless what he's doing at the time. Clearly, motion work is a natural extension of pack expression: obedience must be immediate and unwavering.

Motion training also offers the side benefit of enhancing responsiveness. A dog's obedience often reflects overall improvement after learning one or two motion exercises, particularly in terms of producing a more attentive, quicker worker. The Sit from Motion can improve Automatic Sit at Heel. It can do wonders for a dog who is less than Sit-Stay reliable. The Platz from Motion is practical for its own sake, and is an excellent foundation for teaching the Down on Recall. The Stand from Motion can enhance understanding of the Stay concept.

## MOTION EXERCISES AT HEEL

### Teaching Sequence and General Procedures

When teaching Out-of-Motion obedience, follow the same training progression used for teaching the exercises statically: first the Sit, then the Platz, last the Stand. (This format isn't carved in stone—it's merely a guideline. Too, a trainer need teach only those exercises desired: if the Platz from Motion has appeal but the Sit and the Stand don't, skip them.)

With Out-of-Motion instruction during heeling, technique demands the dog perceive the handler as not having stopped with him. Thus, the animal must already be a super-fast responder to commands, or momentary pressure needed to position him can disrupt rhythm and mar the lesson.

### Sit from Motion

Your dog knows what "Sit" means—it was the first formal lesson in *Dog Logic*'s Companion Obedience program. Still, it's been a while since initial Sit work. Because your companion has been performing the action in terms of *Automatic* Sit at Heel and *Automatic* Front Sit during Recalls, it's likely been months since he's heard the command. The intent of current sessions is to reawaken the response such that when pooch subsequently hears "Sit," he'll react instantly.

On-leash your pet to the training area and allow some sniff-and-explore time. Once his attention is clearly elsewhere, command, "Sit." If he responds quickly, praise, "Good Sit," and reinforce intent with "Stay." If the response is slow, immediately make him Sit, and command, "Stay."

After a few seconds, move your charge with "C'mon, pup," or a similarly casual direction. Don't use the formal heeling command—we're not working on heeling just now. Shuffle around the training area for a time, allowing if not encouraging your dog's attention to stray again. When it does, repeat the sequence. After three repetitions, take pooch from the training yard, telling him what "Good Sits" he did.

Maintain this teaching pattern until the animal is responding with

Using the leash to enforce the Sit from Motion.

instantaneous Sits. That's all you've directed so far: "Drop whatever you're doing and Sit, right now and right where you be."

Next, incorporate these lessons into heeling. Bring your pal to the training area, and command, "Sit." Assuming the response is not only correct but quick, the next words he should hear are "Good Sit—Fuss." Move out smartly. Seconds later, command, "Sit," and give the Stay signal while stepping away a few feet. Don't stop walking when commanding, "Sit"—take two or three steps before halting. It can be helpful to turn left in front of and facing your dog just as you command, "Sit," backing away a short distance while continuing to give the Stay signal. This deflective action stifles scooting without having to resort to force.

Should pooch fail to respond to Sit during this transfer-to-heeling stage, no need exists for a four-alarm correction—you're probably seeing confusion. A dog well-versed in Automatic Sit at Heel may be bothered by the unexpected change in pattern. "Sit? But you're still moving. You stop and I'll sit. That's how we've always done it." You'll accomplish more with a suggestive leash flick than you would by yanking the lead. True, your pet has known Sit for some time, and you've reinforced its meaning over the past few days, but he's unfamiliar with it in this format. Allow room to adjust to the alteration, and remember that any dog needs at least a blink to respond to a command.

Now the training becomes a matter of gradually increasing the distance you cover after leaving, performing the exercise at a normal pace, and weaning your friend from the Stay hand signal.

## Ponderable Points

Bear in mind a couple of particulars when teaching the Sit from Motion. First, hold the leash left-handed so you can instantly apply any necessitated compulsion. Let the lead slip from your fingers as you depart. Second, hurling the pre-coiled leash behind a sensitive canine immediately after the "Sit" command is adequate correction. The lead's weight, augmented by the throw's velocity, transmits sufficient pressure to convey the message.

## Platz from Motion

Warm up your dog with some quick and lively heeling. During a stop, command, "Platz." Plan to take the animal down immediately should he perform the exercise sluggishly, reminding him that Platz demands a fast response.

Timing is more important than sheer force when enforcing the Platz from Motion.

Again command, "Fuss," and establish a brisk pace. Carry the leash right-handed, with sufficient slack that it hangs just shy of the ground. After a few steps, command, "Platz," *as* your right foot contacts the ground. Then bring your left foot onto the leash. That's how long pooch has to comply: the time it takes for your left foot to come forward and pin the lead. The technique's beauty is if the dog lies down promptly, no force is transmitted because the leash—like the dog—is on the ground. As the animal downs, praise, "Good Platz," and command, "Stay." Keep walking, moving a short distance away. Return, and repeat the drill three times. End the workout after the final run-through to prevent subsequent activities from detracting from the lesson. As with the Sit from Motion, what remains is gradually increasing the distance covered after commanding, "Platz," and fading out, "Stay."

A trap that trainers sometimes overlook is establishing a pattern of a certain number of steps between each Platz from Motion. We're creatures of habit, and I've seen more than one person habitually walk the same number of paces before commanding "Platz." We can argue all day long whether *Canis familiaris* can count—I think he can, to four at least—but I've observed dogs being taught this exercise start to go to ground after the fourth step, for instance, when the trainer has frequently downed the animal every four steps. Remember, dogs are intensely patterned in their behaviors. Don't create faulty communication.

Incidentally, if Schutzhund competition is your goal, though this exercise is normally followed by a Recall and Finish, don't initially practice those elements with the Platz from Motion. This restriction is for the same reason that the Finish, when first taught, is not linked with the Recall: to deflect anticipation.

### Stand from Motion—Medium to Large Dogs

Begin with your dog in the Heel position. Hold the leash right-handed. While walking at a normal pace, command, "Wait," and simultaneously apply light, left-hand fingertip pressure to the left flank. Don't grasp the flank—merely touch it. The method stops most dogs in their tracks.

Be sure to apply the procedure to the left (outside) flank, not to the one nearer you. Touching the inside flank can cause a dog to move his hindquarters away from the handler, a reaction that would defeat the goal of an instantaneous Stand from Motion.

It's usually not necessary to remain next to the dog once he's halted, but initially do so if he seems unsure or nervous about this development. As he stops, reinforce intent with the Stay hand signal. Don't accompany it with the verbal command, lest pooch react to Sit's "S" sound by Sitting.

### Stand from Motion—Small Dogs

With smaller canines, teach the Stand along a fence or a similar structure adjacent to the animal's left. Because you operate from his right, having an obstacle to his left prevents the dog from shying away.

Warm up with some heeling. Then command, "Fuss" once more and—after a few steps—command, "Wait." At the same instant, stop and slide your left foot under your pal's midsection. (With a tall dog, use your left hand.) Use the instep to position him, not the toe area. The maneuver is difficult, not only from the standpoint of coordination and balance, but because it must be effected smoothly so not to scare the animal. Accordingly, as with several moves presented in my training program series, practice it by yourself until you feel competent to try it with your dog.

With any size dog, looping a second leash around the girth can be helpful in reinforcing Wait. Avoid forward collar pressure, though. That causes a dog to Sit.


## DOWN ON RECALL

### Competition Considerations

This exercise is often taught with an eye toward competing for the AKC Companion Dog Excellent (CDX) obedience title. Usually referred to in that context as the *Drop on Recall,* in which case the handler interrupts the Recall by commanding pooch to lie down when the animal has covered about one-half of the distance, it's best not undertaken before securing the Companion Dog (CD) title. Since CD competition requires an uninterrupted Recall, a dog who has been taught the variation may react incorrectly when in the stressful environment of an actual obedience trial.

However, certain nonconflicting foundational work can be covered prior to CD competition. Specifically, a dog can be taught to Platz from a stationary position at a distance from the handler (covered in chapter 2,

"Hand Signals"), and to Platz from Motion. Then, after earning the CD title, the only remaining adjustment is to merge those lessons with the Recall.

### Down on Recall—Teaching

Increase to twenty feet the distance at which your dog Platzes reliably from the Stand. Then commence the following segment on a textured surface, not a slippery one on which a dog could easily slide when stopping from a run.

Do a long, uninterrupted Recall. Then "Platz" pooch and depart swiftly. Command, "Here," from about thirty paces. As the animal nears the halfway point, walk swiftly toward him while commanding, "Platz," both verbally and via the hand signal. Repeat the commands to the extent needed. The instant your pet grounds, stop in place, exuberantly praise, "Good Platz," and call, "Here," communicating a "What fun!" message. Quickly repeat the entire sequence three times, then end the session. What remains is adjusting the pattern: calling your dog from a Sit, remaining in place as you command, "Platz," and delaying your second "Here" for several seconds.

### Down on Recall—Attitude

A negative aspect of the Drop is that it can teach a slow Recall. Forever a behaviorally patterned animal, a dog may learn there's no need to rush to the handler because he—the dog—will shortly be directed to lie down. One way to maintain a high-flying attitude is to drop the Down on Recall for several weeks once pooch has mastered it. He won't forget the lesson—remember: Dogs learn for life. Practice only straight Recalls for a few weeks, occasionally interspersing the Drop, communicating much exuberance and pleasure as you call pooch the second time.

### The Creeper

There's a direct and convincing correction for the dog who persists in taking extra steps after being commanded to lie down. With a larger animal, go to him and take the animal off the ground by encircling his neck (near the chest) with one arm, and the area just behind his rib cage with the other. Don't grab fur—your hands should clutch only air—vise-lock pooch with your arms. Carry him to the spot where he should have downed, transporting him so that he cannot see where he's being carried.

Thwarting the creeper.

Emphatically place him on the ground (I said *place*—not *slam*), comment, "I told you, Platz!", while pointing at the location, return to your starting point and continue the lesson. The technique is the same with a smaller dog, except that the animal is lifted using your hands along his rib cage.

The effectiveness of this method resides in the fact that the dog, like the cat, abhors being off-balance. He equally dislikes being carried such that he can't see where he's going. More than once I've seen a single application of this correction eradicate creeping habits of several months' duration.

## Reflection

> *'Tis sweet to hear the honest watch-dog's bark*
> *Bay deep-mouth'd welcome as we draw near*
> *home.*

Lord Byron, *Don Juan*

# 6

# Retrieving and Jumping

## RETRIEVING

The picture on page 70 is a scrapbook item, depicting three of my Dobermans on a Sit-Stay. None is wearing a collar, each is holding a dumbbell. When asked, "How in the world did you get them to do that?", I confess it's a temptation to wax eloquent along a theme of "training prowess." Actually, it was simple. I told the male, "Sit," and—under the two females' watchful eyes—gave him a dumbbell. Soon after placing two other such objects on the floor, nature took its course. In fact, there was barely time to grab the camera before the females were each holding a dumbbell. A little positioning, a quick "Sit," and *voila!* A click for posterity. It was a classic example of pack competition *and* cooperation.

### Attitude—Your Pet's

Competitive training is highly productive, especially in building attitude. It can save much teaching time and effort. A similar tactic is working seasoned retrievers where inexperienced dogs can observe. Dogs are motivated not only by competition but by imitation. Untrained animals watching educated ones work is also good distraction conditioning for the performers.

Another attitude enhancer is having your dog carry an article (like

a Nylabone, or a dumbbell) to another person, preferably a family member. Use a closed room, to prevent wandering. With you and your assistant sitting or kneeling several feet apart, hand your pet an object. As he mouths it, encourage through voice and gesture, "Take it to Jerry," Jerry being your assistant. At the same moment, Jerry should commence encouraging the dog to bring the article, praising him as he does so. When pooch arrives, Jerry should take the object, briefly examine it approvingly, then return it to the apprentice retriever while encouraging him to carry it back to you. This simple method strengthens the retrieving habit while building attitude. The dog learns that carrying an object to a person is enjoyable.

### Attitude—Yours

One needn't initiate retrieving from the perspective that a battle is about to be joined. Many retrieving systems seem based on just such a premise, an outlook that can result in a self-fulfilling prophecy. Some authors spend more time illustrating compulsion methods than in acknowledgement of the fact that dogs are born with a drive to retrieve. Blind, unquestioning subscription to harsh teaching styles has taught more than one sound retrieving prospect to fear a dumbbell and distrust the handler. One can adopt any manner of coercion should the need arise. Unless pooch resists, though, don't risk lost animation and rapport by presuming your companion will contest the work. Otherwise, you approach the project with a negative mind-set, which risks transferring a similar attitude to the dog.

### Subtle Compulsion

Having said all that, be aware that compulsion is present in my retrieving program from the onset, though in subtle form. I have pooch wear a pinch collar during teaching situations. The tactile sensation imparted by the device subconsciously reminds that what the trainer says is not to be taken lightly. Thus, effective force is not necessarily overt or active. It can operate via implication as well as through implementation.

### Pre-Training

I begin fetch training by naming objects my puppies encounter. My word for a Nylabone is *bone*. I use the same term to denote a dumbbell. Such associating provides a positive mental link toward the dumbbell

There is retrieving and there is retrieving. Two of the author's German Shepherds, Misty and Hawkeye, peacefully resolving the question, "Who shall fetch the frisbee?"

from day one and, no—I've never had a problem with dumbbell chewing from this *crossover conditioning*. The texture and feel of the two articles is too different.

## Equipment

The dumbbell should be a trifle large and heavy, to inspire a dog to work. Too small and light a dumbbell can induce a less-than-serious attitude. For competition, use a dumbbell that meets the governing body's specifications, but regardless what application you plan, avoid dumbbells undersized in relation to the dog.

# RETRIEVE ON FLAT GROUND

## Prerequisite

Teaching the basic Retrieve on Flat Ground requires successful completion of *Dog Logic*'s Companion Obedience program. My approach to retrieving calls for extending patterns your pet learned during Companion Obedience training. The Retrieve evolves as an individual exercise from work the dog already knows; it's not presented as a new and distinct lesson.

## Teaching the Flat Retrieve—Phase One

Begin the first session with some lively heeling, followed by a Sit-Stay. The purpose is merely to loosen up the animal, to put him in a working frame of mind. Then set your pet up for a second Sit-Stay. This time, though, before commanding, "Stay," and stepping away, make your dog accept and hold a dumbbell. If adequate foundational work has been done, he'll willingly take the object. Should mild compulsion be required, reach across the top of the muzzle and exert upward finger pressure behind the canine tooth. This causes nearly any dog to open his mouth.

Say, "Take It," when presenting the dumbbell. The common practice of a second command, such as "Hold It," is pointless: it tells an animal to do something he's already doing. Also, it can lead to problems—for all a dog knows at this point, "Hold It" means "Drop It," and were he to do so he'd be open to criticism for doing what he may have thought was the right thing.

Too much dumbbell, and too little.

Inserting a finger behind a canine tooth is effective in forcing open a dog's mouth.

Command, "Stay," and leave, going no farther and for no longer than when you first taught the Sit-Stay: a couple of feet for three to five seconds. Return, reclaim the dumbbell, and praise, "Good Stay." Should pooch continue to hold on, *don't* correct him. If he's that interested in keeping the object, so much the better. To cause the release, gently lift one end of the dumbbell, causing it to rotate in a manner (if not at a speed) similar to an airplane propeller. He'll let go.

The key to the initial retrieving lesson is this: Should your pet drop the dumbbell, or even attempt to, you must make him see that the action constitutes a broken Stay for which he'll be corrected. We're linking the hold of a dumbbell with the concept of Stay. Most dogs grasp the idea quickly, as letting go is a form of movement and pooch already knows that Stay means, "Don't move." Now you must show the animal that the command also means, "Don't let go." Should he loosen the bite, instantly apply the *verbal bridge** technique by saying, "No," followed by replacing the article in his mouth. The notion that a premature release is akin to a broken Stay must be made abundantly clear. It may even prove necessary at first to compel the hold by gently grasping your pet's muzzle.

Practice the technique four times a session. The goal is not endurance—a dog should never be required to hold a dumbbell for longer than thirty seconds. When he'll hold it for as long as it takes for you to walk a dozen paces away, count to ten, and return—a level you should reach within a week—it's time to begin the next stage.

## Teaching the Flat Retrieve—Phase Two

The next step is Recalling your companion as he holds the article. Commence this phase when the dog is as reliable holding a dumbbell during a Sit-Stay under distractions as he's when not holding the object.

When first Recalling pooch carrying a dumbbell, revert to initial Recall-teaching technique: calling over short distances as you move backward. During the first few days, use the Here cue. Your companion understands that command, while "Bring"—the Retrieve command—means nothing to him at this point. When the animal is solid on this modified Recall, begin to increase distance and decrease back-pedaling.

*See *Dog Logic,* chapter 8, "First Week."

Sit-Stay while holding a dumbbell.

Step two in teaching the retrieve. Adding the Recall.

## Command Modification

Once the animal Recalls reliably with the dumbbell from fifteen feet, begin calling him with "Bring"—pause a beat and take a step backward—"Here." Once he's responding to "Bring," start phasing out "Here" by gradually softening your voice until the word disappears.

## Environmental Influences

As you increase Bring distance, start working in locations that cause your dog to Recall slightly uphill. Steep inclines serve no purpose, but the added burden of a moderate uphill run causes your pet to work harder. This leads him to concentrate more on the business at hand and less on any residual contention. When pooch will Bring the dumbbell from thirty feet, advance to the next step.

## Teaching the Flat Retrieve—Phase Three

Conduct the following on flat ground, not on an incline.

Begin the day's session with a single, thirty-foot Bring. Then leave your dog on Sit-Stay, taking the dumbbell with you. Set the object on the ground two paces from him while glancing pointedly from him to the dumbbell. Walk two more steps, turn, and face your pet. You should be four paces from your dog, with the dumbbell at the halfway point on a line between you. Point at the object, and command, "Bring." One of seven actions will occur.

> The dog will advance a few steps, pick up the dumbbell, and bring it to you; or,
> he'll grab it and attempt to run away; or,
> he'll Recall normally, *sans* dumbbell; or,
> he'll maintain the Stay; or,
> he'll depart the area, leaving the dumbbell behind; or,
> he'll stand and remain in place; or,
> he'll lie down.

## How to Respond

If he brings you the dumbbell, which will usually be the case, praise, "Good Bring," as he arrives. Let your student know what a good job he did as you end today's session, to guarantee leaving pooch with a sense

Step three in teaching the retrieve: Requiring the dog to pick up the dumbbell.

of accomplishment that any subsequent "lesser-than" performance could override. Don't concern yourself with straight front-sits and the like—premature tinkering with such niceties can lessen confidence—share your pleasure at your pal's understanding, fine-tuning the routine later. Continue this pattern for the next three days, increasing the dumbbell's distance from you and from your pet by two feet daily, and the number of retrieves by one a day.

Should the dog attempt to flee the scene with the article, immediately respond with "No," and encouragement to Bring. Moving backward as you call may be all it takes to draw pooch to you. He's close to doing the right thing here, his only error being one of direction, and sudden flight is probably no more than a doggy version of keep-away or "Let's play!" It's wiser to modify a happy attitude rather than risk dampening it through force.

If your pet attempts to come to you without picking up the object, don't respond with compulsion unless you're absolutely certain he's resisting your intent. That would be a rare case, indeed—seldom will a defiant dog come to the trainer during a disobedient act. Most likely he's mixed up and is trying to do what he thinks is proper. He's partially learned to associate the command "Bring" with coming to you. Thus, doing so without picking up the dumbbell could easily be the action of a canine who is trying to obey. Perhaps he thinks that since you didn't give him the object when you left, he isn't supposed to go near it. This dog's mission is best clarified by leading him to the article, and suggesting through word and gesture that he should pick it up. If he still seems confused, press his head down to the dumbbell, and insert a finger behind a canine tooth to open his mouth. Remove the finger and—as his jaws close on the dumbbell—command, "Bring," as you back away encouragingly.

Should pooch continue to hold the Stay, it's 99 to 1 that he's confused. Repeat, "Bring," while gesturing as needed to move him from the Stay into the desired response.

The animal who runs off isn't ready for this phase. He needs more Stay and Recall practice while holding a dumbbell.

If the dog responds by standing and remaining in place, the problem is confusion, not disobedience. A canine who stands in this type of situation is looking for further direction. Repeat, "Bring," accompanied with gestures and body language to communicate your wishes.

Similar is the animal who responds by hitting the ground. He's obviously confused, and should be dealt with by verbal and gestured encouragement, not by force or disapproval. He's likely been brought too far too fast. Revert to Recalls-while-carrying-a-dumbbell for a few days.

Darryl Dockstader and his Alaskan Malamute, Nick, who seems determined to keep the dumbbell.

### "You Put It There—You Pick It Up!"

If at any point the dog refuses to grab the dumbbell—that is, the animal knows what you want and defies you—you're faced with out-and-out disobedience that should be met head on. Understand: I'm not talking about the canine who asks the owner, "Say what?", or even the pooch whose attitude is, "I'd really rather not." The former is unclear about the owner's intent, and the latter can often be brought around by repetitious application of the finger-behind-a-canine-tooth technique. I'm speaking here about the animal whose message isn't just "No," but, "Hell, no!" Given the work that's preceded this training, it's a rare creature who reacts like this, but if you're absolutely certain that it's your dog we're discussing, proceed as follows.

Grasp the pinch collar's top chain left-handed, and turn your fist clockwise to create pressure. Maintain the correction as you lead pooch to the dumbbell. Don't rush to the object—take your time. You want him to be anxious to get to it next time. While still twisting the chain, push the dog's head toward the article. The instant he contacts it, stop the pressure, and attract pooch by moving backward while encouraging, "Bring."

### Not Yet

For now, do *not* formally command your friend to release the dumbbell. A better approach is praise for bringing it, followed by a sham tug-of-war contest. This is easily instigated by bending or kneeling in front of your pet, grasping the ends of the dumbbell, and acting as though you're having great difficulty taking it from him, complete with resounding grunts, groans and gasps of effort. Don't concern yourself should excitement draw him from the Sit position as he struggles to hang on. The ideal result would be for your pet to wrench the object from you, and bound away with his prize. When you need to reclaim the article to end the session, gently rotating the dumbbell by lifting either end will cause its release. Don't correct your friend should he try to hold on—we don't want to teach a losing attitude. Merely continue until you've wrestled it away.

### Teaching the Flat Retrieve—Final Phase

When your dog will reliably Bring the dumbbell placed between you, take the final step. Put him in a retrieving mind-set by having him Bring it once. Then, with the animal at heel, command, "Stay," throw the dumbbell three or four feet, and command, "Bring." If you sense uncertainty, walk your companion to the object and clarify the mission encouragingly. Should his attitude bespeak, "You threw the thing—you go get it!", the ensuing correction should be the same as outlined for recalcitrance during the pick-it-up-along-the-way lesson.

## AFTER TEACHING THE RETRIEVE ON FLAT GROUND

### A Peripheral Matter

Should your pet grab the object not by the crossbar but by an end, don't worry about the minor technical flaw for now. Once he's retrieving solidly, work on the problem by repeatedly positioning it correctly. Don't verbally chastise pooch *as* he picks up the dumbbell incorrectly—such timing could confuse: "What? Am I not supposed to grab the dumbbell when you say, 'Bring?' " Allow him to take a few steps with the object before adjusting it.

### OUT!

I teach Out ("Release!") in conjunction with the Guard Game (see chapter 3). The command easily transfers from play toys to dumbbells. Teaching Out without first teaching the Game can be accomplished by commanding, "Out," then gently rotating the dumbbell by lifting either end. A tap under the chin is another way of suggesting the release. A determined animal can be taught Out through *steadily increasing* pinch-collar pressure (i.e., pull the leash, rather than yank it). Take care not to apply so much force that enthusiasm for retrieving is dampened.

### "Out!" is a Verbal Command, Not a Signal

Teach pooch that reaching for the dumbbell does not signify, "Out." Otherwise, you risk his dropping the article before you can take it. An effective technique for instilling a hang-onto-it attitude is encouraging tug-of-war games via the object. Another is letting your dog walk among other (friendly) canines while holding his prize. He won't drop it in that setting as he knows that another could pick it up. In any event, sound conditioning includes reaching for the dumbbell, tapping both ends and withdrawing your hands without taking the object. Praise, "Good Bring," as your companion continues to hold on. Should he drop it, confusion is

This is not an end-of-the-world technical flaw, but one which should be corrected before teaching the Retrieve Over High Jump, lest the animal lose his bridgework by striking the obstacle's top board with the dumbbell.

The grasp for throwing the dumbbell so that it's less likely to bounce off-line.

the issue. You'll accomplish more with a gentle "No, No," and replacing the dumbbell, than with compulsion. Then repeat the tap exercise, praising your friend as he maintains possession.

## The Throw

The ideal toss causes the dumbbell to land at a given spot, instead of bouncing to a side. Hold the end between your thumb and fingers. Position your thumb directly behind the block, and curl your fingers over the front, with the knuckles toward the direction you intend to throw. Though it may feel foreign at first, this grip causes a dumbbell to backspin as it sails along. The motion usually causes it to die where it lands. Practice the technique without pooch nearby, lest you have to inhibit enthusiasm by having to restrain him from chasing the object.

It's also wise to rehearse using a lightweight dumbbell. I once saw a handler inadvertently fling the retrieving object straight up. About the time she asked, "Where'd it go?", the thing came down and gave her a resounding whack atop her cranium.

## Adaptation of the Front Retrieve

After your dog has been reliably retrieving for several weeks, make a final pattern adjustment: Show him to turn toward you before picking up the dumbbell.*

One reason underlying this modification regards ring pressure. In many cases a trainer doesn't teach formal retrieving for the fun of it—the intent is to compete. By teaching your pal to perform the retrieve in specific fashion, he'll have more on which to concentrate. Not only does keeping attention focused on the job deflect tension, it has the salutary effect of taking a dog past any lingering contention. Once taught the Front Retrieve, if canine dissension occurs it's in the form of the dog grabbing the dumbbell with his rear toward the handler, instead of not picking it up at all. Another inherent plus of the Front Retrieve is that it can produce straighter front-sits. A Front-Retriever tends to align on the handler before or soon after grabbing the dumbbell.

---

*The Front Retrieve is not incorporated with initial retrieving lessons as that would constitute teaching more than one pattern at a time. It's easier for trainer and trainee alike to modify retrieving behavior once the work is sound overall.

Introduce the Front Retrieve by jogging with your companion during pursuit of the dumbbell, then gesturing that he should go past the object and turn before picking it up, momentarily blocking the dumbbell with your legs if need be. To a degree, the pick-it-up-along-the-way drills have established the concept of facing the handler when grabbing the article.

A related tactic for introducing or reinforcing the Front Retrieve is putting the dumbbell on the ground (instead of throwing it), and blocking the dog's line of approach with a chair or a similar object, positioned so he has to turn toward you prior to picking up the article.

### Use of Stay Commands in Retrieving

AKC obedience rules permit Stay commands (spoken, signaled, or both) prior to throwing the dumbbell. By contrast, Schutzhund forbids Stay cues during obedience.

Use "Stay" during initial retrieving lessons, simply for clarity. Later, when the dog's drive for retrieving is high, gradually delete the "Stay" command from the routine, giving the cue in a progressively softer voice. Facilitate the fade-out through replacement: throwing the dumbbell, then performing a bit of quick heeling prior to sending your pet. That way you interrupt the pattern while heightening attention without using force. Too, it's another way of reminding pooch that your next command can't be predicted. Another technique is to throw the dumbbell, then command, "Platz," prior to directing, "Bring." The principle here is the same—interrupting the pattern. After a few such lessons, your companion will grasp that your action of throwing a dumbbell (or any object) isn't a signal for pursuit.

### A Drive Heightener

The following animation technique may seem somewhat off the wall, but I've seen it work often enough to make it worth sharing. It has to do with inciting and increasing fire toward a dumbbell, and it's often effective with any dog, but specifically with the Sporting breeds (Springers, Goldens, Labradors, etc.).

With your dog on-leash, station yourself near a large tree. After capturing attention by momentarily teasing him with the dumbbell, suddenly slide the object up the tree trunk, starting near the base. You'll have to make a fast read of your pet's interest, because if he starts forward in pursuit you must react quickly by moving the dumbbell tantalizingly

Teaching the Front Retrieve.

out of reach. Then whip the article behind your back in tempting, "Where'd it go?" fashion, and run it up the tree again, this time allowing pooch to grab it as you slide the object along.

The odds are seven out of ten that this procedure will be helpful in raising your hunter's interest. If the basis for the technique's effectiveness is unclear, observe your dog's reaction toward a squirrel as the little creature darts up a tree.


## JUMPING

### Easy Jump-Retrieving Training

You may be able to commence this work simply by tossing a dumb-bell over a jump and commanding, "Hup—Bring." Given the Companion Obedience, jumping-at-heel work and retrieving lessons so far, your pet may respond properly. Still, many trainers prefer to complete foundational steps first.


### Lesson Sequence

The keys to successful agility training are the instruction sequence, and not progressing to the next stage until the dog is proficient at the one before it. The following schedule covers more common obstacles.

| | |
|---|---|
| At Heel | Single Board |
| At Heel | Scaling Wall (Optional) |
| Recall | High Jump |
| Recall | Scaling Wall (Optional) |
| Recall | Bar Jump |
| Directed | High Jump and Bar Jump |
| Directed | Retrieve |
| Directed | High Jump, Bar Jump and Broad Jump |
| Retrieve | High Jump |
| Retrieve | Scaling Wall (Optional) |
| Retrieve | Bar Jump |
| At Heel | Broad Jump |
| Recall | Broad Jump |
| Retrieve | Broad Jump |
| Ring Format | Broad Jump |

Teaching the Recall Over High Jump.

Preventing a dog from coming around a jump.

The first element, jumping over a single board during heeling, is covered in *Dog Logic*'s tenth chapter.

## RECALL OVER STANDARD HIGH JUMP

This exercise heightens Recall enjoyment and animation while teaching pooch to come to you over an obstacle. It's not only foundational for High-Jump Retrieving and Directed Jumping, it has the side effect of speeding up normal Recalls.

### Teaching

Set the high jump at one-third of pooch's wither height. Heel over it a time or two, to put the dog's mind into jumping mode. Leave him on a Sit-Stay about three feet from and facing the obstacle. Step across it (to suggest the correct path), and face your pet, standing within two feet of the hurdle. Slap the top board, command, "Hup," and quickly move backward to attract your friend and provide landing room. If your dog is sound-sensitive, slap the board lightly. If noises excite him, hit the jump a good lick. Command, "Sit," as your companion arrives, but don't be concerned for now if his response is less than perfect. Gradually raise the jump height as the animal develops confidence.

### The End-Around Play

Should a dog attempt to come around the jump instead of over it, he'll usually go around the same end each time. Deflect the problem rather than apply compulsion—force often induces stress and stress inhibits jumping—an anxious canine is reluctant to leave the safety of Mother Earth. Place the end around which the animal cheats against a building, fence, or similar structure, making the end-run impossible. Should your pet react by trying to go around the other end, block that avenue with lawn furniture, or by similar means.

### Use of Compulsion

Rarely is it necessary to force a dog over a jump. If pressure is occasioned, lift the animal bodily and drop him over the obstacle, praising, "Good Hup," as he lands. This is not to say that one should throw or hurl a dog across a jump. Pooch should be lifted quickly and released

Compulsion applied in a situation of stubbornness.

from a safe height, not thrown down. Then immediately direct, "Sit-Stay," step across the jump, and call him again. Once momentum is established, don't stop until pooch has had several successes. Advance to the Bar Jump when he's comfortable with the High Jump.

## RECALL OVER BAR JUMP

### Teaching

This work is not appreciably different from the Recall Over High Jump, save for the obstacle's appearance. Starting at low height, angle the bar across the High Jump's top board. Practice Recalls over this modified jump for four days, starting pooch six to ten feet from the hurdle for this and subsequent stages.

The next step is removing the bottom board, replacing it with lengths of doweling (or dumbbells) on each side, equal to the width of the removed board. This maintains the current working height while creating a visible bottom gap.

A few days later, remove the next board from the bottom, replacing it with doweling equal in length to the combined width of the removed boards. If the dog tries to go under the obstacle, block and shove him back under the jump, then call or lift him over it.

The final step is using the Bar Jump proper, eliminating the boards. Start with bar height equal to the middle of your dog's chest. Raise the bar two inches per session until it's at his correct working elevation. Call pooch from the direction that, if he bumps the bar, it will fall away from the supports without toppling the entire structure, which could injure and frighten him.

## THE DIRECTED EXERCISES

### Teaching the Directed Retrieve

Begin by having pooch fetch a dumbbell, the purpose being to put him in a retrieving frame of mind. Next, have your dog retrieve a cloth glove, first allowing him to sniff and otherwise examine the new article. If the animal shows any reluctance or anxiety toward the object—a highly unlikely response—overcome the problem via play activities with the glove before proceeding.

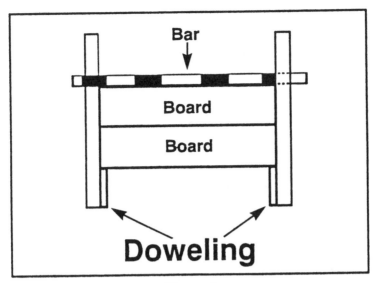

Figure 1

The first step in introducing the Bar Jump.

Steps two and three in teaching the Bar Jump.

Displayed above is my form of compulsion for the dog who insists on going under the bar rather than over it. A trainer who can't perform this technique is working with too much dog.

The final step in teaching the Bar Jump.

Then command, "Sit-Stay," walk four paces in the direction your dog is facing, and place the glove on the ground. Use body language and eye contact to keep attention on you and on what you're doing. Return to the Heel position, point toward the glove, and command, "Bring." If your friend displays any confusion over what's expected, walk him to the article, and communicate his mission through word and gesture. Should resistance cause pooch to hold back—an extremely rare occurrence at this stage—it's probable he's been brought too far too fast. Revert to dumbbell retrieving until the animal is clearly past contention.

Following four days of single-glove retrieving, initiate the following sequence. Begin a session with another placed-glove retrieve. Then command, "Sit-Stay," and go drop the glove once more. Instead of returning, though, drop a second glove a few feet to the left. Return to your pal, command, "Fuss," turn to your left and halt, aiming you and pooch toward the new glove.* Point at it, and command, "Bring."

Most retrieve the correct glove. Presuming your worker is in this majority, praise, "Good Bring," as he returns. Take the glove and segue from approval to, "Fuss," aligning pooch toward the first glove. Then command him to fetch the remaining glove.

Should the dog step toward the first glove, immediately block him with your body, and guide him to the correct article. Should he seem confused, stay with single-glove retrieves for a few more days before initiating the two-gloves modification.

Four days later, set gloves at north, east, south, and west, with your student observing the placements. Direct your UD candidate to retrieve them one at a time. Keep the retrieving order random; avoid establishing a pattern pooch might key on. After a week at this level, install the ring format by working with only three gloves, gradually adjusting the location of the outside two until all are in a line perpendicular to your starting location.

**Directed Jumping and the Send-Away**

In AKC competition, the Send-Away precedes Directed Jumping, but it's better to teach that element separately (see chapter 8), later combining it with Directed Jumping. This allows pooch to master one element at a time. Teach Directed Jumping via an unstructured approach or through

---

*If it's easier for you to do an about-turn in place to face your charge toward the second glove, do so.

First teach pooch to retrieve a single glove.

Block the dog rather than correcting him should he start for the wrong glove.

The next step in teaching the Directed Retrieve is to place gloves at the compass points.

97

one more systematized, depending upon your level of rapport and preference of method.

### Directed Jumping—Rapport Method

With your dog present, erect both jumps, configuring them at low height and setting them ten feet apart. Recall your companion over the Standard High Jump (see figure 2). Do it again.

Then walk your dog to a point between the obstacles and a dozen feet behind them. Aim the animal toward the High Jump, and command, "Stay." Walk to an equidistant spot, relative to the obstacles and the dog (see figure 3). Emphatically point and step toward the High Jump and command, "Hup."

As pooch sails over the correct jump, praise, "Good Hup," and take him back to the starting point. Command, "Stay," return to the location opposite the animal's, and repeat the exercise. Do the routine twice more, then end the session.

On the next day, repeat the preceding exercise once. Then "Stay" your companion, having first aligned him toward the *other* obstacle, the Bar Jump. Return to your command location, and—adding pronounced body language—command him over this second jump. If he does as well with it as he did with the first hurdle—and he probably will—great! Rapport has saved you both a good deal of time and effort. Now the work is gradually raising the jumps' heights, repositioning them until they're eighteen to twenty feet apart, phasing out aligning pooch toward either jump, and starting him from at least twenty feet.

During the teaching sequence, should your pet take any action other than the correct one, *don't* chastise him. Perform some work at which he excels (to finish high), and call it a day. Initiate the *structured method* tomorrow.

### Directed Jumping—Structured Method

Begin by leaving pooch on a Sit-Stay, fifteen feet from and facing a Standard High Jump. Walk to the hurdle's opposite side and command, "Hup." Skip the Finish. Repeat the exercise, but this time move leftward a few feet *as your pet leaves the ground*; turning to face him as he lands. Run through this routine three more times, then close the session.

Start the next period by leaving your dog on a Sit-Stay, fifteen feet from and facing a standard High Jump. Walk to the obstacle's other side,

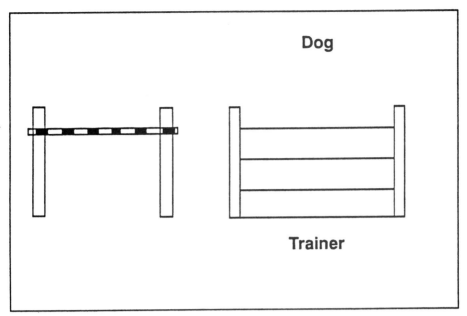

**Figure 2** First position of dog and trainer

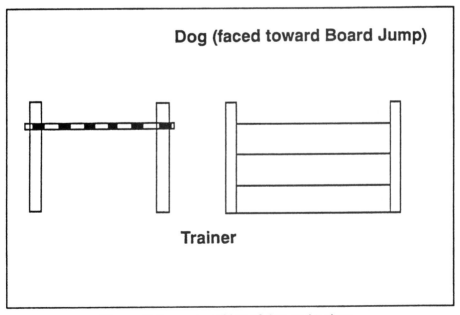

**Figure 3** Second position of dog and trainer

and after standing there for a few seconds, move a few feet to your left. Adding an exaggerated hand signal, verbally command your student over the jump. (Should he attempt to run to you, block him and repeat the "Hup" command while gesturing toward the obstacle. If need be, lift him over the hurdle.) Repeat this new procedure three times before ending the period.

Over the next few sessions, gradually position yourself farther left until you're twenty feet removed from the centerline between the two jumps. Though less distance is required in competition, the *extra-mile principle* operates here by saying to your dog that he's to clear the indicated obstacle regardless how far you are from it.

The next stage is steadily moving your pet's starting point to your left (his right). "Sit-Stay" your friend three feet left of the two jumps' centerline, and walk to a point opposite his new starting position. Adding excessive body language (stepping and pointing toward the desired jump), command, "Hup." Once your pal is handling these modified Recalls Over High Jump, increase by two feet daily the distance by which you are both removed from the centerline between the jumps.

The next step is to replace the High Jump with the Bar Jump. After a few sessions of working exclusively with it, using the same teaching pattern as you did with the High Jump, complete the process by bringing the High Jump back into the picture. At this point your dog should willingly negotiate either obstacle. When first using both jumps, give your directive signals with exaggerated emphasis. Tone them down as your pal becomes comfortable in the work.

### Two Separate Commands

Some trainers use two different commands for the separate jumps: perhaps "Hup" for the High Jump, and "Over" for the Bar Jump. An obvious extension of such logic is that one should use a third command for the Broad Jump, another for the Scaling Wall, yet another for jumping into a vehicle, and so on.

A single command directing a dog to jump over a designated obstacle is sufficient. "Hup" denotes a specific activity, not a particular hurdle. Since UD rules allow a hand signal to signify which jump the dog is to negotiate, use of differing commands seems to be little more than window dressing.

An interesting experiment is to take a practiced directed jumper, and—using a hand signal and a grunt as a command—send pooch over

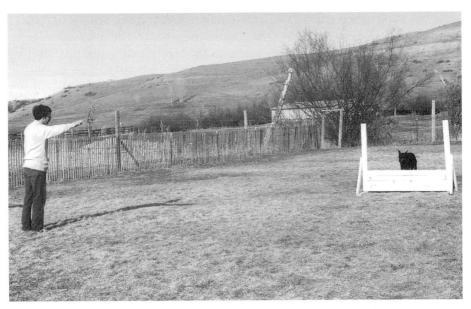

The hand signal indicating the jump to be negotiated.

Teaching the Retrieve Over High Jump is little more than a recombination of previously learned skills.

either jump. You'll find that the dog keys on the signal, not the verbal command. This is reasonable in pack terms, where communication is mostly silent. In the foregoing example, the hand signal points the way; the verbal command starts the dog by canceling the Stay. I've seen more than one titled UD head for the indicated jump after hearing only his name.

### It's the Tone; Not the Tune

Here's a related point to consider. When staging obedience demonstrations for school children, I close by asking my dog, "Do you love me?" He responds by jumping up and giving me a smooch of sorts (see *Dog Logic*'s chapter 13, "Dog Tricks"). The youngsters get a kick out of it, as do I. However, the animal does the same thing if I ask, "Do you hate me?" It's largely tone of voice and body language that cue a dog. Sounds take a backseat.

## RETRIEVE OVER HIGH JUMP

Should pooch be only so-so in any elements of basic obstacle or retrieving training, shore up weak areas prior to initiating the Retrieve Over High Jump. Otherwise, the animal may extend previous problem behaviors into the new activity.

### Retrieve Over High Jump—Teaching

When starting the Retrieve Over High Jump, begin that day's session with a Flat Retrieve followed by a Recall over the jump. If pooch doesn't perform each exercise well, work on problem areas until you're satisfied.

Initiate formal High Jump retrieving by having your dog Sit in front of and facing the Jump from a distance of ten feet. Set the height even with the animal's elbows. Have him take and hold a dumbbell. Command, "Stay," verbally and via the hand signal. Walk to the jump's opposite side, preferably by stepping over it (to suggest the correct route). Position yourself within touching distance of the obstacle. As one flowing action, slap the top board's edge, command, "Bring—Hup," and back away to create landing room. Repeat the sequence three times, and end today's training.

The front-and-facing Sit needn't be perfect today, and omit the Finish for now. Were your pet to make a mistake, you'd be faced with accepting sloppy work versus using compulsion while teaching a drive-based exercise, a lesser-of-evils choice.

The next day, with pooch at heel, throw the dumbbell over the jump, sending him as it lands by sequentially commanding "Hup," "Bring" and "Hup." The first "Hup" sends the animal, and "Bring" should be timed while he's airborne, going for the object. Command the second "Hup" immediately after the dog picks up the dumbbell. Now the task becomes phasing out the commands used only for teaching, waiting several seconds before sending the dog after the dumbbell, and gradually raising the jump to the desired height.

If resistance occurs during this training stage, the message is that the dog's retrieving foundation is shaky and should be strengthened. The animal has been brought too far too fast.

## Competition Jump Height

In jump-retrieving work, the last element to synchronize to the competition setting is the required working height. As a practical matter, I don't jump my dogs at full height until they are fifteen to twenty months of age, depending on each dog's physical status, growth rate, and maturation. It isn't so much the takeoffs that can cause problems, it's the landings, and that young skeleton must be ready to absorb impacts safely.

## Competition Rules

Significant differences exist between AKC rules governing the Retrieve Over High Jump and those of Schutzhund. As stated earlier, the AKC allows "Stay" prior to throwing a dumbbell but Schutzhund does not. Schutzhund's restriction is more realistic, as the act of throwing something shouldn't be a signal to give chase. In the real world, it could be that the object pitched away is harmful.

The AKC permits but a single command for sending a dog, such as "Bring," "Hup," "Fetch" or "Over." Schutzhund regulations allow two commands: one for the activity of jumping, and a second for the Retrieve itself. Thus, a Schutzhund handler may command, "Hup," and then command, "Bring," while the animal is airborne, going for the dumbbell. This makes more sense than does the AKC's constraint. When a handler commands, "Hup," he's said nothing about retrieving. Similarly, when a handler commands, "Bring," he's giving no command to jump. True, dogs learn the pattern, but that doesn't negate the rule's inherent fuzzy logic.

As the AKC occasionally alters required jump heights, be sure you have a current rule book. One meter (39.3 inches) is the jump height for all Schutzhund entrants, regardless of breed or size. As a Schutzhund is a protection dog (*schutz* in German means "protect"; *hund* means "dog"), the rationale for this requirement is that a canine who lacks sufficient size to clear a one-meter jump isn't likely to be effective in strong guard work.

## Jump Colors

Competition jumps are white. However, I've seen CDXs, UDs, and Schutzhunds balk at nonwhite jumps. It's worthwhile to condition using obstacles of various colors, as well as jumps having boards and support posts of different hues. While other than white jumps shouldn't be encountered in competition, by using unique colors your companion will be more thoroughly trained and better able to deal with conditions beyond the ring ropes.

## Don't Forget This Aspect of Conditioning

As part of AKC jumping, the judge measures each dog's height at the withers, "with an ordinary folding rule or a steel tape." Accustom pooch to being approached and measured by strangers, lest the procedure cause nervousness at a show. To ease your dog into the routine, start by having family members and friends known to your dog do the measuring. Later, gradually use helpers new to your companion.

Don't reward with tidbits for reacting properly to the procedure. A food-reward policy can teach a dog to expect food when he's being measured, which can distract him from the job at hand.

## THE BROAD JUMP

### The Simplest Obstacle?

Though many training manuals present this section prior to Utility's Directed Exercises, I prefer to teach it last, or nearly so. The Broad Jump can be one of the more deceptive requirements in terms of simplicity. It appears uncomplicated on paper, but its true ease lies in how many ways a dog can misperform it. Thus, delay teaching the Broad Jump until your pal is an experienced jumper.

Use various styles and colors of jumps as part of your pre-show conditioning process.

Condition your dog to the fact that he'll be measured in the ring.

## Broad-Jump Configuration

During initial teaching, arrange the jump as a stacked formation: two boards placed horizontally on their edges, parallel to one another and eight inches apart; two boards set horizontally on their flat sides, atop and at slight angles to the first two boards. This beginning layout is intended for all dogs, except for members of the Toy Group, the Bichon Frise, and the Lhasa Apso. If your pet would be more likely to crawl over this setup than jump it, alter the configuration to one less tempting.

## Broad Jump—Teaching

The first segment, taking pooch over the Broad Jump at Heel, is no different from heeling over any new obstacle. "Fuss" toward the jump and command, "Hup," as you both leap over it, praising your student with "Good Hup" after landing. Repeat the Over-Broad-Jump-at-Heel procedure three times before progressing.

Next, Recall your pet over the formation. For the first few days, don't alter the jump's setup from that used for Over Broad Jump at Heel. After four days of Broad-Jump Recalls, commence lengthening the Jump's dimensions a few inches daily, eventually extending it to the correct length and configuration. For reasons that will become clear, after leaving pooch in preparation to commanding him over the Jump, always walk along the obstacle's right side, relative to the animal's starting location.

The last step is to format the exercise into the manner in which it's performed in the CDX ring. The handler leaves his dog on a Sit-Stay facing and at least eight feet from the Broad Jump. He then walks to a point along the right side of and facing the hurdles. When cued by the judge, the handler commands pooch to jump, turning toward the landing area while the dog is airborne.

Adapt the procedure via two simple steps. First, following a Recall over the hurdle, set your dog up for an encore. Command, "Hup," but this time—as soon as he's in the air (not before)—hurriedly back leftward into position alongside the hurdles, facing the spot where your companion will land. The purpose in this movement is to avoid inadvertently giving your dog the momentary impression that you are running at him.

After a few days at this level, take the second step. Conduct the exercise once, as you've been doing. Then Stay your pet for a repeat performance. Leave, but instead of moving to the jump's opposite end

Bill Zeigler and Lacotah, UD, demonstrating the Broad Jump exercise. This super, working Golden was the first dog Bill had trained. That they took High-in-Trial honors at their first show demonstrates that an excellent trainer and a good dog is a hard combination to beat.

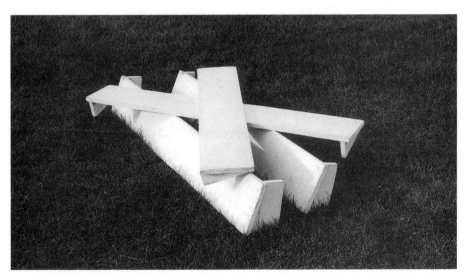

The idea behind initially configuring the Broad Jump as shown is to prevent your dog from learning to walk through it, a habit that's difficult to eradicate later.

The first step in teaching the Broad Jump is heeling your dog toward the obstacle, which is in a stacked configuration, and jumping over it with him.

The next step in teaching the Broad Jump is Recalling your pet over the obstacle, lengthening its dimension a few inches daily until it approximates the full distance your dog is required to jump in the ring.

and turning to face the animal, command, "Hup," *as you're passing the right edge of the hurdles.* Accompany the cue with a sweeping, directionally suggestive gesture with your left arm. Now the task becomes a matter of gradually altering the procedure into one in which you first halt at the jump's right side prior to commanding, "Hup," and phasing out the signal.

## Anticipation Problems

Anticipation difficulties, such as jumping before commanded, can be eliminated by preceding "Hup" with an infrequent and unexpected "Platz." Command your partner to lie down while he's in the Sit-Stay, then send him over the Broad Jump. Another ruse is leaving the dog in a Sit-Stay at the end of the jump, and—after walking to the obstacle's right side—return without commanding, "Hup," and heel away. The intent common to both methods is to break the pattern, saying to your pal that he must wait for your cue; that your next command cannot and should not be predicted.

## The Walker

The greatest difficulty in teaching the Broad Jump is had by the trainer whose charge has learned to walk across or through the hurdles. From a dog's perspective, the Broad Jump would be more easily negotiated by walking through or over it. The High Jump (and, to a degree) the Bar Jump suggest a need for levitation. The Broad Jump doesn't. This is why Broad Jump work is better taught only to a reliable jumper.

To eradicate the problem, first drop the exercise completely for several weeks or even months, depending on the difficulty's severity and duration. This lapse causes as much extinction of erroneous memory traces as possible, which is preferable to trying to override them while they're fresh and strong. Then restart the training, using a new method and a different command. Using the former command can trigger old habits.

## To Achieve Centering

A second Broad Jump difficulty is that a canine may jump toward a front corner, often the one nearer the handler. The upright-post design

The leash is a useful tool in many instances.

Why not?

110

of the High Jump, as well as the handler's location relative to the obstacle, usually drives a dog to jump center. The Broad Jump's center definition is more vague.

Off-center jumping can usually be trained out simply by placing a leash across the corner being cut (most dogs won't jump over their own lead). Accompany placing the leash with much deliberate movement and eye contact. Another helpful device is temporarily placing High-Jump supports at both sides of the Broad Jump's midway point. This helps define or at least suggest the Broad Jump's centerline.

### The Extra-Mile Principle

Another extension of the extra-mile principle (mentioned earlier) is—though it's not required by the AKC or Schutzhund—teaching retrieving over both the Bar Jump and the Broad Jump. Such thorough training falls under the heading of leaving no pebble unflipped, as does using the Broad Jump for a Directed-Jumping obstacle. In a phrase, such tactics can't hurt.

## THE SCALING WALL

This obstacle is used in Schutzhund retrieving. While it's not part of any AKC routine, I recommend teaching the Retrieve Over Scaling Wall even to dogs who won't be competing in Schutzhund. The activity builds confidence, and it can enhance the retrieving fire of AKC competitors. This additional training can only help serious workers, as can exposure to window jumps, fence hurdles, barrel stacks, and teaching dogs to jump over each other. If yours is a small dog, merely scale down the wall's dimensions.

### Configuration

A Scaling Wall can be visualized as two seven-foot by four-foot sheets of plywood set on a two-by-four frame and hinged together at one end. When set up, a triangle effect is created. The Wall's apex is adjustable from nonexistent (flat on the ground) to about six feet, depending on the angle of positioning. Three wooden two-by-two rungs are fastened horizontally to each side of the Wall, to facilitate climbing. Measuring from the peak, they are positioned at twelve, twenty-four, and thirty-six inches.

The Scaling Wall.

Jump training is limited only by imagination.

113

The Scaling Wall is not just for Schutzhund.

## Acclimating

Introduce puppies to the Wall when they're beginning to walk on-leash. If you're working an older dog, the familiarization methods are essentially the same as those recommended for pups.

Locate the Wall upon a flat, grassy area. Setting it on a hard surface may cause it to undulate as you walk across it, due to minor structural imperfections. Such shifting could startle a dog, causing the animal to associate anxiety with the obstacle.

As the two of you first approach the Wall, make no comments or gestures intended to draw attention to it. At this point, the less heed you pay it the less chance your pet will be concerned with the new and unfamiliar surface. Should an inexperienced animal seem concerned or uncertain, don't force him onto the structure. Doing so could heighten nervousness. Sit on the Wall, perhaps even stretch out on it, and encourage pooch to join you. His anxiety will pass in time. Gradually raise the incline over a period of several weeks. As you increase height, continue to walk on and over the Wall with your pal.

## Retrieving Over Scaling Wall

The procedures for teaching the retrieve over this obstacle are similar to those used in the Retrieve Over High Jump. Begin with Recalls Over the Wall, initially maintaining a low angle. Then advance to retrieving as outlined in the "Retrieve Over High Jump" section, gradually increasing the Wall's angle as your companion becomes proficient at the work.

# THE ABORTED RETRIEVE

## Rationale

Teaching an aborted retrieve is prudent. That statement may horrify some, but the purpose is control. Should pooch pick up something he shouldn't have, it might take too long to get to him to take the article away. Of course, don't practice with dumbbells, scent articles, or in a simulated ring setting, but with sticks, play toys, and similar objects. Further, teach the Aborted Retrieve only to solid retrievers. To introduce the idea to dogs new to retrieving is to court disaster.

## Teaching Method

Have your dog hold a play toy* while sitting at Heel. Command, "Out," but don't reach for the article. Should pooch fail to drop it, repeat the command to verify that confusion isn't the issue ("Out" is usually accompanied by you reaching for an article). If the animal still won't release—moreover, if his bearing says, "No, I flat won't do that"—flank-correct him. (The flank-correction is described in chapter 3, "The Guard Game," under, "Compulsion Basis of the Out Command.") As he drops the toy, immediately reward by throwing it for him. The next several sessions are carbon copies of this one, except to increase distance from the dog gradually until he'll reliably release at one hundred yards.

The next objective is to have pooch drop the play toy while he's in motion. Deal with compliance or noncompliance in the same fashion as when commanding "Out" during a Sit-Stay. At this stage add the commands, "Leave It—Fuss," meaning, "Leave the toy's location, and return to the Heel Position." Teach this by directing, "Out—(*pause*)—Leave It—(*pause*)—Fuss." The idea in having your pet return is so that—in a real situation—you can remove him from the "Drop It!" circumstance and maintain control. As the basis for this command is compulsion, correct the dog should he fail to come to you. Once he's returned, reward your pal's Leave-It response with permission to Find It. Most dogs like to Find It. There's also a discernable Spillover Effect into Scent Retrieving in terms of increased drive and positive motivation.

## Reflection

> *My little old dog:*
> *A heart-beat*
> *At my feet.*
> Edith Wharton,
> *A Lyrical Epigram*

---

*The reasoning behind using the play toy is that, if a dog will relinquish *it* at a distance, given his great attraction to the object, he's likely to respond similarly with any article.

116

# 7

# Scent Retrieving

## Overview

Scent retrieving is fetching a handler-scented article from among several similar but unscented objects. Commonly referred to as *Scent Discrimination*, the phrase is somewhat misleading as the unscented articles are just that: bereft not only of handler scent, but of any other as well. True scent discrimination has each item bearing a unique odor, instead of just one article being scented.

Many who have never taught Scent Retrieving approach the work with a measure of anxiety. Novice students, after watching a dog demonstrate the Scent Retrieve, often react that it must be extremely challenging to teach. Many Utility Dog trainers with whom I've visited, though, feel the work is usually easier to perfect than precision heeling. Amen.

Should UD competition not be among your goals, I still encourage you to teach this exercise. Sniff work can not only be a good deal of fun, it can further illuminate canine ways and capabilities. Too, if you enjoy getting a rise out of your friends, watch their reactions the first time you run your pet through the exercise. It'll knock their socks off.

Competitors: Scent Discrimination can be taught to untitled animals without causing confusion over performance of pre-UD requirements. However, it shouldn't be shown to a dog not solid on the Retrieve on Flat Ground and the Retrieve Over High Jump. Also, scent work should not be taught concurrent with teaching Directed Retrieving, Directed Jumping, the Send-Away, or Tracking. The "whys" of these restrictions concern the notion that we want to be working with a seasoned, "all-aspects" retriever, but we don't want to risk confusion with other "Go away from me" exercises like the Send-Away, or similar yet different nose work, like Tracking.

Choice of teaching method depends on the dog's bonding level and how he best learns. The first approach offered is based only on rapport and is loosely structured. The second is more systematized, and though rapport still plays a part, it does so to a lesser degree. Some dogs more readily assimilate sequential information when it's presented in a highly blueprinted format. Others do just as well—often better—by diving into the middle of things.


## SCENT RETRIEVING—RAPPORT METHOD

Because dogs are drawn more to articles of nature than to manufactured items, start by placing six twigs (bark chips work equally well) in a four-foot-by-four-foot area.* Wear scaled, rubber, kitchen gloves when handling the articles to avoid scenting any, and position them so none touches another. Put one of the objects inside your shirt to scent the item thoroughly, and go leash up your pet.

When the two of you arrive at the training site, heel to a point ten feet from the nearest article. After pooch's Auto-Sit, command, "Stay," and withdraw one of the scented objects from your shirt. Capture attention by flipping the item in the air a few times. Pass it once under pooch's nose, remind "Stay," and walk to the unscented articles. Place the scented article peripherally near the others such that you can be sure of its location. Return to your dog, briefly put your hand near his nose, then command, "Find It," while gesturing encouragingly toward the articles. Repeated "Find Its" and gestures to get pooch moving are permissible.

As your companion approaches the objects, follow slightly behind. You need to be nearby, but not so close as to distract. When nearing such curious things, almost any dog lowers his head to examine them. (The dog who shows scant interest should be encouraged via voice and gesture to do so; he shouldn't be forced.) As he inspects the items, softly praise,

---

*It's preferable to work on a surfaced area, rather than a lawn, which can emit distracting scents.

"Good." Should he try to pick up any article other than the correct one, gently intone, "No, No," while guiding him from it. When your retriever eventually sniffs the right one—regardless whether he reacts to it—instantly respond excitedly, "Good Find It—Bring!"

At this point, every dog to whom I've taught this exercise via the rapport method has done two things. First, he jerked his head up and looked at me, exhibiting what I call the *Moment of Recognition:* that flash when a dog's aspect says, "Eureka! I see what my trainer wants!" After my "Good Find It—Bring!" response to his wide-eyed, searching look, the animal has done the second thing—grabbed the object, and proudly walked toward me.

Pet your companion, telling him what a Good Find It he did, and walk him from the training area, allowing him to carry his prize if he wishes. End the session at this point to guarantee finishing high, which would be at risk were the routine repeated. When you do Out the article, use only minimal force in taking it should pooch fail to release when commanded. Don't chance dampening enthusiasm through compulsion.

After three training sessions like the foregoing, switch to placing the scented object among the others *prior* to bringing your pet to the area. A week later, change to using ring articles by substituting them for whatever items you've been using. Should you meet any resistance to the formal articles, inserting them inside individual, cloth gloves can make the objects more canine-acceptable. Then follow the program outlined in Step 5; "Conclude Transfer to Ring Scent Articles," under the following "structured method" for Scent Retrieving.

## SCENT RETRIEVING—STRUCTURED METHOD

### 1. The Seek-Back

In her booklet, *Find It! A Complete Guide to the Scent Discrimination Exercise,* Margaret English insightfully spoofs the simplicity inherent in teaching the Seek-Back.

> Then all you have to do [to show in Canada] is teach him the seek-back, which you can do while you're gassing your car on the drive up there.*

---

*Margaret English, *Find It! A Complete Guide to the Scent Discrimination Exercise* (New York: Margaret English Publications, 1985), p. 20.

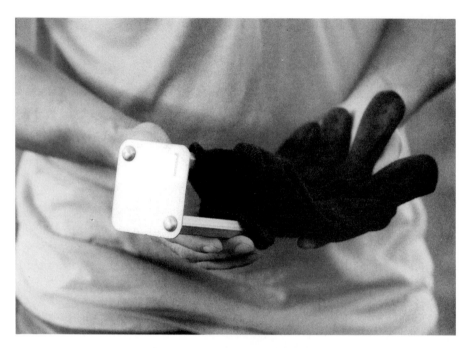

An article-in-glove combination.

Initiate teaching the Seek-Back by placing four cloth gloves inside your shirt to scent them heavily. Without letting pooch know that you have the gloves, bring him to the training area, and briefly warm up with on-leash heeling.

Should the heeling not be up to par, straighten out the problem, take pooch from the training yard, and start the Seek-Back tomorrow. It's unproductive to follow compulsion with teaching fresh material—doing so risks prejudicing the dog's attitude toward the new activity.

If the heeling is acceptable, continue in a straight line, and drop a glove behind you as you walk. Do so right-handed, with your pet unaware you dropped anything. After three or four paces, turn around, continue walking, and bring your hand under the animal's nose. As a continuation of the same motion, command (repeatedly, if needed), "Find It." Adding any necessary gestures, lead your retriever toward the dropped glove.

As he approaches and perhaps sniffs, investigates, and pounces on the article, praise, "Good Find It," and encourage, Bring. Don't worry if the front sit is less than perfect—deal with such minor flaws later, concentrating for now on the larger picture. Command, Out, pocket the glove, and continue heeling.

After several more paces drop another glove, again without your charge being aware you've done so. As before, take a few more steps, turn around, bring your hand under his beak, and command, "Find It." Praise, "Good Find It—Bring," take the article, and continue heeling. Repeat the entire procedure twice, then take your pet from the training area, marveling at his splendid Find Its. The next three training sessions are repeats of this one.

## 2. Begin Transfer to Ring Articles

The following step adds ring articles, beginning with metal ones. If a dog resists a Utility object, he generally does so via the metal items, not the leather ones. It's better to deal with any rebellion now, not after a preference for the leather articles has been established.

Effect the transfer through one of two ways, depending on which approach you feel will be easier for your pet. The first is inserting a metal article into a scented glove and continuing with Seek-Backs. The second is to simply commence using the metal articles in place of gloves. Such a step might appear to offer unwarranted haste to the progression, but some very successful trainers claim it's the only way to go.* If you make the transition to ring articles directly, immediately modify the approach by inserting the articles into gloves should use of the new items confuse your dog. Conversely, should he decide that he's simply not going to pick up "that thing," be it article or article-within-glove, correct as you would during any retrieve refusal.

Remain for four days at this level: four 6- to 15-foot, daily Seek-Backs of metal, glove-enshrouded scent articles, or of the metal scent objects alone.

### 3. Pre-locate Articles

This step constitutes a minor yet significant change. Place four gloved (or plain), scented articles twelve feet apart in a straight line *prior* to bringing pooch to the training area. Tell him, "Find It," as you enter the site, leading him toward the first article. This modification takes you one step closer to formal Scent Retrieving.

### 4. Addition of Unscented Articles

If you've already eliminated the gloves, ignore references to them in the following outline.

Several days prior to starting this phase, set out three gloves and three metal articles to air, to eliminate any residual scent they may harbor. Wear scalded, rubber, kitchen gloves when handling them, to avoid inadvertently scenting one.

Days later, create a fourth article-in-glove combination, after first scenting the retrieve article and the glove heavily. Tuck the package in your shirt, and don your kitchen gloves. Gather up the three non-scented, article-within-glove combinations, taking care not to touch them bare-handed. Proceed to the training area, *sans* dog. Arrive from a direction other than the one you'll follow when bringing pooch, the idea being not to lay a scent trail he could key on.

Once there, place the unscented articles in a triangle, each eighteen inches apart. Set the scented article/glove two feet from the unscented ones, creating a diamond pattern. Locate it so that wind currents don't carry scent from it to the unscented items. Remove your kitchen gloves,

---

*Personally, I'd just as soon go for broke with a full scent layout (and have been known to do so) as to risk confusion in the training sequence, but this gets into the area where only you can know your pet's tendencies best.

fetch your dog, and escort him to the yard. As you do, remember that a behavior you must be able to read is the phenomenon referred to earlier as the moment of recognition: that beat in time when a dog's behavior suddenly radiates, "Aha! I understand!" During the next few minutes, your interpretive skills are going to get a workout.

Walk your pet toward an unscented article. Send a message down the leash by making the approach akin to stalking prey: crouched, sneaking along slowly and deliberately, encouraging your dog *sotto voce* to investigate and to Find It.

As pooch nears the first non-scented combination, doubtless he'll sniff it. If he doesn't, in fact, make certain you haven't leashed up the family cat by mistake. Keep still as he scents, so not to distract. He'll either turn away, or attempt to pick up the article. Should he turn away, say a prayer of thanksgiving, and guide him toward the next unscented article, continually urging, "Find It."

Should pooch start to pick up a non-scented article, prevent him from doing so. Allow a couple of sniffs, then move him along before he has an opportunity to pick up the object. If he tries to pick up a non-scented combination before you can move him from it, block him, or—if you're too late—command, "Out," physically taking it from him if need be. Remember that when a dog investigates something in this type of instance, he normally sniffs it, stares at it for a blink or two, and mouths it if he feels like picking up the object. It's during that second or two of staring that you must guide him from the non-scented article.

At the second non-scented article, your pet may begin to exhibit confusion. Having not met with success, he may be unable to see what's expected of him. If you sense any canine bewilderment, skip going to the third unscented article/glove combination. Proceed instead to the scented one, encouraging as before, "Find It."

As you arrive at the correct (scented) article, position yourself so your dog can see you without having to turn from the object (so not to strain his concentration). Watch very closely as his nose goes down. Be alert for that moment of recognition. While it's sometimes very subtle, the phenomenon is often characterized by the animal suddenly freezing all motion, after first snapping his head back slightly from the article, then by either looking at you searchingly (for confirmation), or by literally pouncing upon the object. In either case, your response must be emphatic and sincere: "Yes! Good Find It!" Add, Bring, if pooch seems unsure whether to grab the article.

After a few moments, escort your dog from the area, allowing him to carry his prize if he wishes, and commenting along the way how impressed you are with his "Good Find It." End on this obvious high point, rather than risk overriding it with less successful experiences that might occur were you to continue. Give yourself some kudos, too. You've accomplished much.

Continue this training sequence for the next three days, each day placing the scented article in different locations relative to the unscented ones. Don't inadvertently teach pooch to home in on a visual pattern.

## 5. Conclude Transfer to Ring Scent Articles

Begin this reduction phase after four consecutive successful days of your student retrieving scented, article-within-glove combinations. Using scissors and imagination, the objective is to reduce the glove's size gradually. Start by snipping off the fingers. Over the next few sessions, cut off a bit more until only wrist bands remain.

Once the gloves have been trimmed down to little more than wrist bands, avoid any scent work for a few days. During the layoff, concentrate on some activity your dog truly enjoys, such as the Guard Game. The idea is to take his thoughts further from specific memories of scent articles in combination with gloves. Then return to Scent Retrieving where you left off, except that you should no longer use gloves or portions thereof.

Four days after restarting, add the leather articles. Four days after that, incorporate wooden ones if you want more thoroughness in training.

## 6. Format Routine to Ring Specifications

Effect three modifications over the next few weeks. First, begin grouping the articles together (but no closer than eight inches, the minimum AKC distance). Second, gradually increase the distance pooch must cover to the articles until he's starting from forty feet. Last, condition your pet to sit quietly at heel while a helper moves behind you, playing the role of a ring official placing a scented article among the non-scented ones. (The helper should use tongs to handle the article you've scented.)

## VARIATIONS

### Number One

Occasionally a trainer may encounter a dog who is perfectly willing to perform any task, but who simply doesn't grasp the essence of Scent

Retrieving. If that describes your pet, make one subtle adjustment in the training program: initially teach the animal to seek his own scent. The approach can be used with either the rapport or the structured method, as follows.

First, when a dog experiences uncommon difficulty with any exercise, drop the work for several weeks to allow fading of unproductive memory traces. In this specific instance, to get past any negative carryover effects pooch may have experienced with formal ring articles, begin the new approach using matched wooden dumbbells.

Have your dog retrieve a dumbbell on flat ground four times. This loads the object with his scent and yours. Leaving your companion in a Stay, hide the article several yards away, either in tall grass, behind a tree, among some leaves, or under a shallow covering of snow. The purpose is to prevent your friend from seeing precisely where you placed the object. Return to your dog, heel to within a few feet of the dumbbell, and command through word and gesture, "Find It."

Be alert for the moment of recognition. Praise, "Good Find It," as he picks up the dumbbell. Take the object, command, "Stay," hide it again but in a different location and command, "Find It." Repeat this hide-the-dumbbell—Find-It drill twice more, and end the session. If he's so inclined, allow your companion to carry his trophy as the two of you depart the training area. The next three training periods are duplicates of this one, including having pooch formally retrieve the dumbbell three or four times at the start of each session. Use the same dumbbell throughout these practices, to saturate it with as much scent as possible.

Begin the next phase by placing two similar dumbbells three feet apart prior to bringing your dog to the training area. Wear scalded, rubber gloves when handling the items so not to transfer your scent to them. Walk your best friend to the training site, and have him fetch the dumbbell you've been using. When you throw it, though, hurl it directly away from where you've placed the other dumbbells. Out the object, command, "Stay," and place it within three feet of the dumbbells set out earlier. Return to your dog, attach the leash (for control), and direct, "Find It." Be alert for the moment of recognition.

As your companion inspects the items, softly praise, "Good." Should he try to pick up a dumbbell other than the correct one, gently intone, "No, No," while guiding him from it. When your retriever eventually sniffs the right one—regardless of whether he reacts to it— instantly respond excitedly, "Good Find It—Bring!"

Pet your dog, telling him what a "Good Find It" he did, and take him from the training area, allowing him to carry his prize if he wishes.

End the session at this point to guarantee finishing high, which would be at risk were the routine repeated. When you do take the dumbbell, use only minimal force should pooch fail to release when commanded. Don't chance dampening enthusiasm through compulsion.

After three similar training sessions, switch to placing the scented dumbbell among the others *prior* to bringing your pet to the site. A week later, change to using ring articles by substituting them for the dumbbells you've been using. Should you meet resistance to the formal articles, inserting them inside individual, cloth gloves can make the objects more canine-acceptable. Then follow the program outlined previously in step 5, "Conclude Transfer to Ring Scent Articles."

**Number Two**

A good friend had breezed through the first two levels of AKC Obedience competition with his Golden Retriever, earning High-in-Trial honors their first time out. When it came to Scent Retrieving, however, the dog simply didn't get the message.

It occurred to my friend to accent the target article's scent level. He did this by rubbing a piece of bologna on the object dumbbell, then likewise smearing the meat on his hands. As he told me later, "I let the dog sniff my hand, walked him to the articles, he sniffed the one I'd polished with the bologna, and you talk about *Moment of Recognition*! His eyes seemed to bug out of his head." They went on to earn the coveted UD title without mishap.

**Reflection**

> *A dog starved at his master's gate*
> *Predicts the ruin of the state.*
> William Blake, *Auguries of Innocence*

# 8

# Send-Aways

In A SEND-AWAY routine (also called a *Send-Out* or a *Go-Out*), a handler directs his dog to run from him in a straight line until commanded otherwise. Comparative descriptions of the exercise as practiced in AKC Utility and Schutzhund follow.

### Send Outs: AKC Utility vs. Schutzhund

The AKC Utility Send-Away is performed in conjunction with a second exercise, Directed Jumping (see chapter 6, "Retrieving and Jumping"). With his pet in the Heel position, a handler commands the dog away. As the animal nears the ring's opposite side, the handler commands, "Sit." The handler then cues the dog to return over one of two dissimilar jumps: the High Jump or the Bar Jump. After clearing the signified hurdle, the dog Sits in the front-and-facing position, Finishing when commanded. The exercise is repeated, but this time the dog returns via the jump that wasn't used the first time.

UD Send-Outs are never greater than fifty feet. In Schutzhund, the highest competition level is SchH-III. Send-Away distance for those dogs can be a football field in length: three hundred feet.

The Schutzhund Send-Away begins with the dog in the *basic position*: sitting at heel. The handler commands, Heel, the team begins walking, and after ten or so paces, the handler commands the Go-Out. As the animal drives ahead, the handler stops and stands in place. When the dog has covered the required distance, the handler commands him to lie down. He then walks to and counterclockwise around the animal, assumes the Heel position and commands, "Sit." This completes the team's obedience phase of the trial.

At first glance, one might conclude the foregoing routines are two similar applications of the same exercise. In people terms that's so, but it's a truth of a kind. To a dog the two Send-Aways are very different, both in concept and orientation.

In AKC competition, the ring setting is essentially constant from show to show. The dimensions, jump placement, location of the steward's table, and so forth, vary only slightly within a general scheme of sameness. At indoor shows, the Send-Away is usually performed on matting laid out to suggest the exercise's direction and termination point. Rings are clearly separated from spectators by scissor gates, stanchions, or ropes.

By contrast, Schutzhund Send-Outs may be conducted on a football field, in a pasture, or at any similar site. A Scaling Wall, Blinds, Jumps and other equipment may or may not be present. Spectators are near the field, but often there's no clear line separating viewing area from trial field.

## Competition Commands

If you plan to show in both Utility and Schutzhund, beware the potential for canine confusion. Being the behaviorally patterned animal he is, a dog can confuse the manner in which the exercises terminate, especially when working in the stressful surroundings of a show/trial.

An overall procedural difference between Schutzhund versus AKC is that the former forbids using the dog's name with commands while the latter does not. Though I seldom recommend using the dog's name with commands, using the name in Utility just prior to the Sit command raises the odds a dog won't mistakenly hit the ground in Schutzhund fashion. Likewise, using only the command (Platz) at the Schutzhund Send-Out's termination point can clarify the dog's mission.

## THE TARGETED SEND-OUT (AKC-UD APPLICATION)

Because AKC competition demands structured consistency, my method of teaching the UD Send-Away is to target the dog on the ring environment itself. This necessitates creating a ring setting at your training site. That's not to say you must replicate a UD ring, complete with judge, steward, fencing and crowd. If need be, clothesline strung between two trees to represent one side of the ring can suffice.

The two jumps should be present, but they shouldn't be set up during this teaching stage. They're merely equipment on hand, waiting in jumbled heaps to be erected. Don't draw attention to their presence; that could distract from the business at hand.

Locate the best Go-Out termination point in your contrived ring setting. This spot is midway along the side having the fewest distractions. Then make note of your starting point, which is directly across the ring from the termination point. Use a leather or cloth collar for today's training. The Send-Away is based more in drive than compulsion, and at one point we'll be trying to convince your dog to pull you along, as you'll see in a moment. Obviously, a dog would be disinclined to do so while wearing a pinch or a choke collar. Stuff a tennis ball or two in your pocket, attach a tab to the collar and heel on-leash to the ring, proceeding directly to the starting point.

Leaving pooch in whichever Stay he's most reliable, remove the lead, and walk to the ring's opposite side. With much ado, place your jacket (or other outer garment) on the ground such that your dog can easily see it. Return to your pal, point at the target, command, "Run," and quickly escort him to it. Should curiosity drive him to drag you to the object, so much the better. An inquisitive attitude facilitates training.

During your approach to the discarded article, hold onto the collar tab. Convince your friend that he's being restrained from going ahead to investigate. While the purpose is to cause your pet to drive forward, leave the technique alone if you feel it might inhibit. As you reach the "right" distance from the garment—which is that point where the dog's curiosity is as high as it's likely to get—release pooch, simultaneous with again commanding, "Run," and pointing toward the article.

After the animal arrives at the target, allow a few seconds investigatory time, then command, "Sit." (Permit this exploration period only during the first session; prevent subsequent investigations by commanding, "Sit," upon arrival.) Immediately produce the tennis ball—ostensibly from within the target article—command, "Guard" (assuming pooch knows the Game— see chapter 3), and throw the ball for him. The purposes are to show the dog what fun it is to dash to the target, and that he's wise to rivet attention on you upon arrival: to be ready to play the Game.

Praise as your pet returns with the ball, repeat the entire sequence three times, and take him from the area. Encourage him to carry the toy, but don't force the issue. Should he drop it along the way, appear not to notice; keep walking. Don't formally correct the dog if he tries to recover the ball—just keep moving. (Allowing a dog to drop and recover an object *ad infinitum* keeps him from learning the importance of maintaining possession.) The next three sessions are identical to this one.

## Should Matters Go Awry

Some problems that can arise, and how to deal with each, are outlined below.

". . . heel on-leash to the ring," but today's heeling is a disaster. Solution: Get the animal's mind right about Fussing, take him from the area, and try again tomorrow.

"Leaving pooch in whichever Stay he's most reliable, walk to the ring's opposite side." Problem: The dog significantly breaks the Stay. Solution: Correct him. Make him hold the Stay as you proceed to the ring's other side. Return after a few seconds, praise, take him from the yard, and initiate the Go-Out tomorrow.

". . . release pooch, simultaneous with commanding, 'Run,' and pointing toward the article," and the dog's response is to stand there and stare at you. Solution: Run him to the garment, using encouragement rather than force. When the two of you arrive, command, "Sit," and continue the sequence.

"Once the animal arrives at the target, allow a few seconds investigatory time, then command, 'Sit.' " Problem: Your pet has forgotten the meaning of Sit. Solution: Refresh his memory through correction, and continue.

"Immediately produce the tennis ball . . . and throw the ball for him." Problem: The dog moves slightly from the Sit-Stay in anticipation of chasing the ball. Solution: Forget it. It's too minor an infraction to bother with at this point. Toss the toy and continue.

"Praise when your pet returns with the ball." Problem: He doesn't return. Solution: Encouragement. The difficulty is rarely encountered if the Game has been properly taught.

## Changes

After completing the first four training sessions, near-term goals are two. First is to Send-Out the dog without having to walk him as far as the day before. The second is commanding, "Sit" and "Guard," at ever-increasing distances.

To accomplish the first objective, simply stop walking at successively farther distances from the target. Should your pet respond by going part way and stopping, confusion is more likely the problem than defiance. He may be wondering why you didn't run the distance with him as before. Stepping forward and giving encouragement is a better solution than compulsion. However, if pooch resists you, grasp the collar tab and correct via a series of quick jerks accompanied by "Run—Run—Run," while gesturing toward the target. Reattach the pinch collar if needed. Likewise, if at any point your pal would have you believe that "Sit" is foreign to his experience, let him know through appropriate compulsion that you aren't buying it. That type of canine amnesia rarely arises from confusion.

Once your pet will Go-Out unaccompanied to the article, make the following adjustment. Drape a small, easily visible cloth over the ring rope above the target, making certain the activity isn't lost on your dog. Return and carry on with the lesson.

After four sessions, make another change. Set out the clothing article and the cloth target prior to bringing your pet to the training site. Four days later, stop using the clothing article altogether, but continue to hang a small piece of cloth over the ring rope prior to bringing your companion for training. Starting four days after that, reduce the size of the cloth over a period of days until it ceases to exist. Also, during this period-of-the-shrinking-cloth, erect the jumps to pooch's current working height. Setting up the equipment should take place over several days (i.e., a little bit at a time) and without your dog present, to avoid calling any special attention to the jump's presence.

Add *Directed Jumping* (see chapter 6, "Retrieving and Jumping") when pooch is solid on the Send-Away. Once you've integrated the two exercises, play the Guard Game after he takes the first jump. Later, play it after he's jumped both obstacles. Keep moving the Game along until you're using it after leaving the ring area.

When practicing the entire routine, alter which jump you first send your pal over. Don't teach a pattern of always commanding him over the Bar Jump first, for example. That can cause ring problems if a judge initially directs using the other jump.

## THE SCHUTZHUND GO-OUT

I teach my dogs that "Run" means to go away from me in the direction I point so to be in position to pursue the ball I'm about to throw. This is easily communicated by commanding, "Run," while pointing the direction you intend, then hurling the ball in that direction. As your pet catches on, he'll take off as soon as you point the way and command, "Run." Delay hurling the toy a beat longer each day, throwing it so it passes directly over pooch's head while he's in full flight and lands in front of him.

After several weeks, modify the game by commanding, "Platz," after the animal covers a significant distance. Then hurl the ball only after your friend is on the ground. If at any time he backslides, such as slowing down before the "Platz" command, revert to throwing the ball well past him. This makes pooch speed up, lest he feel left at the starting gate as the toy bounds away.

As your dog begins to perform the exercise well, make three sequential changes. First, after the Platz, walk to and counterclockwise around him, aligning yourself in the Heel position. Produce the toy and command, "Guard." This teaches your pet to look up expectantly as you arrive, an attitude judges like to see. Then second, after a week of the foregoing pattern, move the Game further along in the sequence by delaying it until you've commanded, "Sit." Later, play the Guard Game only after heeling your charge several paces from the Send-Away's termination point.

## A Variation

Another method for teaching the Schutzhund Send-Out is dropping a play toy every twenty steps while heeling your dog across a large area. After covering one hundred feet, turn about and command, "Run," running with him to the first play toy. You may also have to run with him to the second one, but it's doubtful he'll have to be led to the third. The message is that another toy is always out there. Gradually increase the distance between toys until only one remains, placed three hundred feet from the starting point.

## Perspective

Two keys to teaching any obedience pattern are patience and consistency. Trainers who maintain this thought, along with the perspective that a Send-Away is little more than a Recall in reverse, experience little difficulty.

## Reflection

A dog is not "almost human" and I know of no greater insult to the canine race than to describe it as such. The dog can do many things which man cannot do, never could do and never will do.

John Holmes,
quoted by Donald McCaig in *Nop's Trials*

# SECTION II

# Specialized Topics

# 9

# Competition

---

## The Right Dog, Revisited

Prior to hitting the competition trail, heed the message of *Dog Logic*'s second chapter: "Start with the right dog." That animal is trainable, willing, drawn toward teamwork and—most important—constituted to handle the stress of working near crowds of people and hundreds of other dogs.

Like you and me, every dog has strong and weak points. The pooch who minds well around the house, but who becomes increasingly stressed around other animals or large throngs, just isn't right for competition. More to the point, competition isn't right for him. To put that creature in an overpowering situation is more than unfair, it's cruel.

Several breeds are more amenable to obedience competition than are others. Attend a few shows and you'll soon note note which breeds excel. Moreover, note which ones don't. Also, study AKC annual statistics covering working titles won by each breed. While it's obvious there are always exceptions, such research is most enlightening.

## Perspective

A sad phenomenon I've observed more than once concerns lost perspective. A person has a devoted, obedient dog. After a few shows in which pooch doesn't do well, the owner recognizes that his pet doesn't have what it takes to handle competition stress. That's where the story should end, with the owner seeing that—though he may not have a High-in-Trial candidate—he's blessed with the company of a loyal, loving friend.

But the cheerless truth is a person sometimes comes to look down on the dog, seeing what isn't instead of what is. Forgotten is the joyful greeting at workday's end, the comforting presence during times of crisis. Ring scores take on a distorted importance they were never meant to signify, ultimately becoming of greater worth to the gung-ho competitor than unconditional affection. Bonding weakens as a gulf widens, ardor withers and more is lost than any ribbon could ever replace.

Scores are fleeting and transient, but a dog's love is forever. Accept and cherish it. In all situations, a sound canine does his best. He may not always succeed in pleasing the owner, but it won't be for lack of trying. In the end, trying is all that any dog—or any human—can do. When an animal doesn't measure up, too often it's from an owner's unrealistic expectations.

As stated in *Dog Logic,* "As I said: perspective. Hang on to it." It's vital, for both of you.

## Obedience Classes

An intrinsic relationship exists between success in the ring and obedience classes. The reason is that, when one aspires to compete for working titles, the support and help received through a professional obedience class can be a godsend. Many instructors have shown successfully, and are more than willing to share their expertise. They not only can assist with the ins and outs of competition, they can help students maintain perspective.

However, I'd be less than candid were I not to mention that unhealthy class settings—rare though they be—can be nightmarish. The following thoughts are offered to help competition aspirants locate worthwhile class instruction.

Obedience classes reflect their instructors. Most are sincere, knowledgeable people motivated by an honest desire to help others learn how to establish control over and rapport with their dogs, and to facilitate successful outings for owners interested in competition. Yet in isolated cases, egotism and ignorance validate the Peter Principle, producing resentment and fear. Unlike a veterinarian, obedience trainers/instructors are generally not required to be licensed or certified.

Yet, like a vet, a trainer can mark a dog with long-lasting, harmful effects.

Dog clubs, AKC affiliated or otherwise, frequently offer classes conducted by the group's trainer. More often than not, that's just what you're looking for. Keep in mind, though, that a club is essentially a group of people with a common interest in the world of things canine, but with varying motivations underlying those interests. The AKC does not test, endorse or certify instructors. There exists the subtle inference that instructors affiliated with AKC clubs possess great wisdom and knowledge about dogs, but sometimes the person who teaches is little more than the group's dominant personality.

Please understand: My intent isn't to put the knock on AKC classes, *per se*. I do feel that many concern themselves overly with the Companion Dog routine, and that they take too long to cover a limited amount of material, but these are minor objections. My purpose is to make aspiring competitors aware that simply because a group has decided to call itself an AKC club doesn't foreordain that its leadership or members know anything more about *Canis familiaris* than anyone else does.

Ask to observe a training session before enrolling. If the sponsors are unreceptive, that's sufficient indication they're well avoided. If you're allowed to attend—hopefully the group will encourage your interest—arrive with and maintain an open mind. You may observe disciplinary actions that appear harsh on the surface, but in reality are proper to the situation. (Leave pooch home. You'll be able to better concentrate on the proceedings, and it's unfair to ask a group to tolerate the presence of an untrained dog who could be a threat to others.)

However, it may happen that you'll encounter instructors who present little more than a power trip. Such people often try to intimidate dogs and owners alike, are frequently righteous and all-knowing, and can emotionally scar a canine for life. I've witnessed dogs being strung up (suspended at leash's end) for merely gurgling at a stranger who attempted to force the animal into submission seconds after making his acquaintance. Such people are generally those who've read (but not understood) one or two training books, and have attended a few seminars conducted by and for the like-minded. The result is cyclic, self-sustaining ignorance. While such a person may have titled a dog, he or she has yet to "train" one. Should you find yourself in the presence of such an individual or group, heed the advice of the Monks of New Skete.

There are some instances when you should simply quit class and walk out. If an instructor "hangs" a dog, swirls a dog around on the end of a leash, kicks a dog (except to stop a real dog fight), insults a handler, consistently refuses to answer questions, or derides the dogs, quit.*

In judging an instructor's worth, consult the following list of questions, offered by Dietmar Schellenberg in his excellent book, *Top Working Dogs—A Training Manual*.

> Does your dog approve of him?
> What kind of rapport exists between the instructor and his own (demonstration) dog?
> Does the instructor teach the dogs, or the owners?
> Can the instructor instruct?
> Does the instructor explain?
> Is the instructor responsive, flexible?
> Is the instructor tolerant?
> Is the instructor knowledgeable?
> Can the instructor handle a critical situation?†

My belief is that a skillful instructor shares rather than controls, guides rather than directs. He or she is intolerant of canine abuse and long on patience in dealing with owners. In any case, be very, very careful in your judgments before handing your leash to anyone. You are *never* obligated to do so, regardless of the setting or the "rules." If in doubt, don't. Your pal is counting on you.

## AKC OBEDIENCE TITLES

### General Highlights

The AKC offers three levels of Obedience competition: Companion Dog (CD), Companion Dog Excellent (CDX) and Utility Dog (UD). CD is interchangeable with the term Novice, and CDX work is referred to as Open. Utility is Utility.

Titles must be earned consecutively. One cannot compete in Utility before earning the CDX degree. Similarly, the CD title must have been attained prior to trying for CDX.

---

*The Monks of New Skete, *How to Be Your Dog's Best Friend* (Boston-Toronto: Little, Brown and Company, 1978), p. 33.
†Dietmar Schellenberg, *Top Working Dogs—A Training Manual* (Webster, NY: D.C.B., 1985), p. 30.

Competition is open to all AKC-registered canines in good health. A dog who is lame, blind, deaf or similarly afflicted, will be excused from the Obedience ring. Further, a bitch in season cannot be exhibited.* Whether an animal has been neutered isn't a consideration.

To earn a qualifying score, or *get a leg,* in AKC-Obedience argot, one must secure at least 170 of the 200 points available. Additionally, more than half of the points for each exercise must be taken. Scoring 15 points in a 30-point routine is not a qualifying total; earning 16 or more points for the same routine is.

To earn an obedience degree a dog must qualify under three different judges—i.e., one must attend at least three trials, though the successful outings needn't be consecutive. For example, if you qualify at two shows, bomb during the third, fourth and fifth attempts but qualify during the sixth, you have the title.[†]

During the individual routines, you, your dog and the judge are in the ring by yourselves, save for the ring stewards during activities requiring their presence. After the dog-handler teams complete the individual exercises, Stays are performed in groups, each group being referred to as a *class*.[‡] Unless excused by the judge, all exhibitors must return for the Stays, regardless of each team's performance thus far.

The judge directs each exhibitor through each exercise. Before every routine the judge asks, "Are you ready?" Every exercise ends at the judge's pronouncement, "Exercise finished." Though no dog may be picked up, they may be praised between exercises. Since dogs must be under "reasonable control"[§] while being praised, do so lightly while in the ring. Animated praise can excite, and the dog who responds by jumping on the handler is not considered to be under "reasonable control."

Using the dog's name with commands is allowed, and Stays may be commanded using both voice and hand signal. Heeling, Recall, Finish

---

*While not advocating showing females in heat (because of the stress it could cause them), the often-heard rationale for the restriction—that it would disrupt other animals—makes no sense. If the presence of a female in season can bag my pet's obedience, he or she needs work.

[†] It's for this reason that certifications should reflect the number of shows required to complete a title. In the foregoing example, the degree should state, "Companion Dog—6." This would reflect the truth of the matter: The dog's reliability is operative about one-half of the time.

[‡] A large class may be divided for the Stays.

[§] *AKC Obedience Regulations,* amended through January 1, 1990; chapter 2, "Regulations for Performance and Judging" (section 22, "Praise").

and Open Retrieving and Jumping commands may be given verbally or by signal, but not both.

Each title's requirements are as follows:

*Companion Dog (CD)*
Heel On-Leash and Figure Eight
Stand for Exam
Heel Off-Leash
Recall—Finish
Group Sit-Stay—One minute
Group Down-Stay—Three minutes

*Companion Dog Excellent (CDX)*
Heel Off-Leash and Figure Eight
Drop on Recall
Retrieve on Flat
Retrieve Over High Jump
Broad Jump
Group Sit-Stay—Three minutes (Handler out of sight)
Group Down-Stay—Five minutes (Handler out of sight)

*Utility Dog (UD)*
Hand-signal Routine
Scent Discrimination
Directed Retrieve
Stand from Motion
Send-Away and Directed Jumping

## AKC Rules Booklet

Be certain you have a current rule book, and that you are well-versed in its contents. A copy of the rules-and-regulations booklet can be obtained by writing:

The American Kennel Club
51 Madison Avenue
New York, NY 10010

**Easy Does It**

During heeling, the judge directs the handler, "Forward," "Right Turn," "Left Turn," "About turn," "Fast," "Slow," "Normal" and "Halt," though not necessarily in that order. About-turns are always made to the right.

When making turns, speed changes and stopping, do so smoothly. I've seen handlers react to a judge's directive to "Halt," for instance, by nearly toppling forward from abruptly slamming on the brakes. Respond to instructions promptly, but smoothly, naturally.

**Don't Rush**

When practicing the Novice Stand, habitually command Stay from the Heel position. AKC rules allow reasonable time to position the dog physically. To simplify the task, a handler often bends next to the animal. That's fine, but often through nervousness or inexperience, after the animal is set up the handler commands, "Stay," and leaves before standing up in the Heel position. That's incorrect procedure, for which points may be deducted.

A second Stand-for-Exam aspect is that when leaving your pet, step away *no farther* than six feet before turning to face him. Also, when making this turn, do so to your left so as not to block your dog's contact with you, as could happen were you to turn right.

After directing the handler, "Stand your dog and leave when ready" (or words to that effect), the judge approaches the animal, pets him, steps away, and advises, "Return to your dog." Since any dog who shows shyness or aggressiveness is scored zero, your conditioning program should include having strangers play the judge's role. Remain next to your pet the first few times, backing away slowly over time until you're at least six feet from him. Should pooch be continually apprehensive about being approached and touched by strangers, *do not* chastise him, verbally or physically. That can make the problem worse. Slow conditioning to a level your pet can handle. Start with having family members and friends known to your dog play the judge's part.

**For the Right Reasons**

Make sure your pal's Recall attitude is good. Although the Recall is initiated by command, pooch should be seen as performing out of a sense of receiving permission to be with you. He should cover the distance

This is a no-no. Judges want to see an exhibitor stand in the Heel position when giving the Stay command.

quickly, arriving in a state of alertness. The rules state, "Substantial deductions shall be made for a slow response . . . failure of the dog to come at a brisk trot or gallop"* My thought is that the exhibitor whose pet responds hesitantly, with head down and tail plastered, should be disqualified. It's true that some breeds characteristically respond in a less-than-fiery manner, and allowances should be made for the fact. Still, the animal who comes in whipped-dog fashion has learned to respond "correctly" for all the wrong reasons. I tell you these things because others—judges among them—share my thoughts, and a timid or fearful Recall can not only cost points, it can influence a judge's overall perception.

An easy method for heightening Recall attitude is having several helpers form a corridor several feet apart, and Recalling pooch through the center while your assistants clap and cheer, "Good Here, Good Here!" To be effective, the people assisting you must be able to radiate sincere approval. They should begin applauding the instant your pet comes out of the Stay he was holding when you summoned, "Here." Periodic conditioning along these lines can raise attitude markedly.

### The Stays

Don't stare at your dog during Stays. Occasionally glance his way, but avoid locking eyes. Your pet may be feeling stress, and a staring contest can heighten discomfort and lead to movement.

Keep your praise light after a Stay, especially the Sit-Stay. I've seen handlers praise to the point of exciting their dogs after the Sit-Stay, knowing that the Down-Stay was next on the agenda. The result is a zestful animal who now has to bury his fire to hold another Stay. Make the upcoming work easier for pooch by keeping him calm and settled. Save your praise for after you've left the ring.

As with the CD routine, the final two requirements for CDX are the Sit- and the Down-Stay. Unlike Novice, Open requires handlers leave the ring after commanding Stay. The times are three minutes for the Sit and five for the Down. Whether you're in active title pursuit or are seeking thorough training for its own value, build up the times of the Stays over several weeks. Overtrain, with goals of five minutes sitting, and fifteen minutes Platz. Unless your dog has some issue with the work, one or two Stays in each position per training session is adequate.

*AKC Obedience Regulations, amended through January 1, 1990; chapter 3, "Novice"(section 11, "Recall, Scoring").

Heightening Recall attitude through mass approval.

## Between Exercises

At the end of each AKC routine, the judge advises that the exercise is completed. He or she then directs the handler to move his dog to a given spot to begin the next routine. Don't heel your pet to the location; tell him something like, "C'mon, pooch." Reason: Should your dog heel badly while being moved, the judge may notice it. True, you're between exercises, and in theory no points can be deducted. Equally true is that some judges may find a way to reduce your score based on what they see between exercises. Moral: Don't do anything in the ring that you don't have to do.

# SCHUTZHUND OBEDIENCE

### General Characteristics

The more widely known Schutzhund titles are SchH I, SchH II, and SchH III. Like AKC competition, titles must be earned sequentially. Unlike AKC showing, the dog must be proficient in tracking and protection in addition to obedience.

One hundred points per trial phase are possible, with 70 needed to qualify. As there are three facets to each trial, a total score of 300 points is possible. Unlike AKC competition, a Schutzhund degree is earned by a single qualifying performance.

Schutzhund trials are traditionally outdoor events. The obedience phase is held wherever a secure, preferably level, large area can be located. Weather is of little concern. I once exhibited in ten inches of fresh snow, and I've visited with handlers who've competed under far more severe conditions.

There are several procedural differences between showing in Schutzhund and AKC. A primary dissimilarity is that a dog need not be a purebred to compete in Schutzhund, nor must any participating animal be registered. Each Schutzhund exercise begins and ends with pooch in the *basic position*: sitting at heel. Except for the Send-Away, hand signals aren't allowed. Using the dog's name with commands is forbidden. The lead must be attached to the choker's dead ring, and the leash must be carried left-handed. Normally, all routines are handler-directed.

Heeling is performed in a pattern, showing all turns (right, left and about), and speed changes (normal, slow and fast). About-turns are performed to the left, toward the dog, who must circle behind the handler in returning to the Heel position. The Heel command may be repeated to initiate any speed changes. The handler's arms must swing naturally during heeling.

Following the on-leash heeling pattern, the dog-handler team heels through and among a moving group of at least four people. After leaving the group, the handler removes the leash while still in motion. Handler and dog then heel off-lead through the group. One stop must be performed during each pass through the group. After leaving the group the second time, the heeling pattern is repeated off-leash. At least two gunshots are fired following off-lead heeling within the group.

During all Motion Exercises, after commanding Sit, Platz or Stand, the handler must continue straight ahead without hesitation or looking back. A command to Stay is not permitted during the Long Down, the Motion Exercises or prior to throwing a dumbbell during retrieving.

Two separate commands, such as "Hup," and "Bring," may be used during obstacle retrieving. If a "Bring" command is used, it must be given while the dog is airborne over a jump or climbing a Scaling Wall. The one-meter (39.3 inches) jump height is the same for all entrants. The Scaling Wall's height is also constant—six feet at the apex.

Use of multiple commands for the same element may result in a maximum penalty of 20 percent per exercise. That is, a handler may give the same cue several times to perform given work, and lose no more than 20 percent of the routine's points.

At least six weeks must lapse between earning a particular title and competition at the next level.


## SCHUTZHUND OBEDIENCE REQUIREMENTS

*Schutzhund I*
Heeling Pattern On-Leash
Heeling On-Leash in Group
Heeling Pattern Off-Leash
Heeling Off-Leash in Group
Sit from Walking Motion
Platz from Walking Motion
Recall—Finish
Flat Retrieve
Retrieve Over High Jump
Send-Away
Sit from Down
Long Down–Stay—Handler at 40 Paces

*Schutzhund II*
Heeling Pattern On-Leash
Heeling On-Leash in Group
Heeling Pattern Off-Leash
Heeling Off-Leash in Group
Sit from Walking Motion
Platz from Walking Motion
Recall—Finish
Flat Retrieve of 2.25-pound Dumbbell
Retrieve Over High Jump of 1.50-pound Dumbbell
Retrieve Over Scaling Wall
Send-Away
Sit from Down
Long Down-Stay—Handler at 40 paces

*Schutzhund III*
Heeling Pattern Off-Leash
Heeling Off-Leash in Group
Sit from Walking Motion
Platz from Running Motion
Recall—Finish
Stand from Walking Motion
Stand from Running Motion
Recall—Finish
Flat Retrieve—4.50-pound Dumbbell
Retrieve Over High Jump—1.50-pound Dumbbell
Retrieve Over Scaling Wall
Send-Away
Sit from Down
Long Down-Stay—Handler Hidden from Sight

## National Schutzhund Clubs

Three national Schutzhund organization are DVG (the German Working-Dog Sports Organization), Schutzhund USA, and NASA (North American Schutzhund Association). The trial rules governing each contain minor format variations for otherwise similar routines, and the title requirements of each differ slightly from one another. For more information, the clubs occasionally run ads in *Dog World Magazine*, often in the breed sections for German Shepherd Dogs, Doberman Pinschers, and Rottweilers.

# COMPETITION GENERALLY

## Perspective

Competition showing can range from amusing and enjoyable to downright nerve-racking. The quality of one's outing depends on two factors: preparation, and—to return to a theme expressed earlier in this chapter—perspective.

I don't try to do better than any other contestants. My students and I concentrate on doing our individual best, period. That's likely one reason why we do place first so often—we're not distracted by other exhibitor's achievements. Sure, we're aware of what's going on, but we're focusing solely on our time in the ring, not on anyone else's. When overhearing ringside comments such as, "I sure hope I can beat so-and-so this time," it occurs to me that the speaker is making a nest for frustration to roost, and will probably transmit a goodly amount of nervousness to the dog. Why? Because the person's focus is misdirected, away from the job at hand and toward a situation over which he or she has no control—e.g., how any other competitor fares in the ring. If someone else scores 200, great! I'm happy for him. A lot of hard work has obviously paid off. Now, having made that acknowledgement, it's time for me to redirect my concentration to the reason for my driving all those miles to get to this trial.

Pets shouldn't be used to meet human ego needs. Doing so puts them in an impossible, no-win situation. Instead of comparing or fixating on scores or placings, compete against the performance you feel can be achieved that particular day. You and your companion are after a qualifying total—anything beyond that is gravy. You should know better than anyone what you and your pal can do, and you should be equally aware of how you've done. The rest is commentary.

Another facet of my competition philosophy is that—while it's been some years since one of my dogs has bombed—I know the possibility always exists. That's part of showing. When one of mine has struck out, I found my sleep wasn't affected, and the sun still rose in the east the following morning.

Many of us have seen a handler take a poor performance out on his or her dog. Indeed, in every endeavor some folks are there for all the wrong reasons. An exhibitor who needs a vent for frustration over a blown performance should start and end with a mirror. It is he who trained the dog and he who entered into competition. Pooch wasn't given a voice. If one honestly feels that landing on the animal several minutes after the fact will improve future performances, that individual should learn something about dogs and seek professional help for himself.

## Pseudo-Competition

Attend as many obedience matches as you're able. Because they simulate many of the trappings of formal trials, matches represent ideal conditioning for the madhouse effect that trials can radiate. Attend only correction matches, where ring corrections are permitted. Some matches forbid corrections, and are therefore useless and even detrimental to training—a dog can learn he won't be made to mind in a ring setting.

If you live in a remote area, the nearest match may be an annual affair held several hours distant, a circumstance that doesn't greatly help your cause. However, it may be that a 4-H (or similar) dog program meets nearby. If so, the instructor may allow you to attend to get your pet ready for the ribbons. An offer to help with the project could pave the way, and you may find enjoyment in such involvement.

## A Mini Fun Match

An effective form of conditioning is performing under the direction of a helper acting as judge. You get practice responding to directions, and your dog gains reinforcement that he's to listen only to you. While recently helping a friend prepare for a show circuit, I directed "Finish," following her pet's Recall. Before she could command her dog to heel, the Sheltie executed a beautiful flip Finish. The animal was keying on me, anticipating the command.

Periodically delay your response to helper directives. In the case above, I advised the handler to ignore my directions sporadically, to let me repeat myself several times before complying. The idea, of course, was to teach pooch that he should respond only to his handler, not key on the pattern or on anyone else.

## Distractions, Distractions

The more distraction conditioning you do the better you'll show. An excellent training location is near school playgrounds during recess. Straight sits and the like are important, but the primary emphasis should be maintaining your dog's concentration. If pooch is well-schooled in the routines, and if you can capture and hold attention in high-stress environments, you should experience little difficulty in competition.

For a fuller discussion of distraction work, see chapter 1, "Part I—Distraction Proofing"

## Remember: Dogs Are Behaviorally Patterned

Don't practice exercises in a consistent order or frequency, lest your pet learn the patterns so well that he becomes bored and inattentive, or anticipates your next move. Always make your heeling turns the same way, and command using constant pronunciation, but vary the sequencing of the routines themselves.

## Negating the Boiler Factory Effect

Prior to showing, gradually accustom your pet to hearing commands in louder tones than he's used to. At a show you may have to raise your voice to be heard over the tumult. If you wait until ring time to acquaint your companion with this fact, your sudden change in volume could inhibit or confuse. Radios and television sets blaring during practice can be helpful in teaching pooch to concentrate on listening only to you.

## Additional Assistance

If you've not competed before, locate folks who have and ask their help. Such people can be a great resource. They've been there. Further, if you've never attended an obedience trial, do so prior to entering. See if the circus looks like it's indeed for you and yours. Leave pooch home when attending as a spectator. Only dogs entered for competition may be on the grounds.

## It May Seem Obvious, But . . .

Enter a dog when he's ready and not before. If that seems to belabor the obvious, keep your ears open the next time you're near a working ring. You'll frequently overhear variations on the theme, "I hope my dog's ready," and, "I just don't know if he's ready or not." Don't enter a trial to find out if you and pooch should be there. Determine that long before mailing the entries.

## Know the Rules

The number of handlers possessing little more than vague notions of what to expect in the ring is astonishing. Hearing a novice exhibitor exclaim to a judge, "You mean now we have to heel *without* a leash?" serves to remind me why I've never harbored more than a passing interest in judging. I feel no envy for the judge's lot. Officiating at AKC and Schutzhund fun matches and 4-H shows has strengthened my resolve never to do so again. Such service causes me to feel much admiration for those dedicated souls who undertake the challenges.

## Be On Time

That heading says it all. Understand, though, promptness is more than a courtesy to the judge, it's a requirement. I've seen more than one handler breeze in with an "I'm here now" attitude, only to learn that his number had already been called, he had been marked absent and he wouldn't be allowed to compete. If you have a ring conflict, which can happen when a handler is required to be in a conformation ring and an obedience ring at the same time, most Obedience judges will do their best to work you in when they can. Get permission from the Obedience judge beforehand, though, or you may be in for a letdown.

## Ring Nerves

Telling an exhibitor, "Now, don't be nervous when you get in the ring," is like telling a child not to be afraid of the dark—it doesn't work. So long as the condition isn't chronic, "ring nerves" is a natural condition akin to "stage fright," one that passes with time and experience. The state to guard against is that which upsets one to the degree that anxiety is transmitted along the leash. Chances of success then decrease markedly.

## "I Wuz Robbed!"

Question: Do judges cheat? Answer: I've not experienced it. To put that statement in perspective, remember that the topic is obedience rings, not conformation arenas. Most Obedience judges are considerate, helpful people who prefer their classes do well. Some may be tough or easy on an entire group, but exhibitors generally receive uniform treatment. It's true that one judge may deduct more or fewer points for the same infraction than another, but that's a problem of the system. If you and your dog successfully perform the routines in accordance with the rules, you're likely to qualify every time.

## You're Being Graded, Too

The sport of obedience is a team effort. Your actions, as well as your pet's, are being judged. That's why score sheets include a *deduction* section captioned, "Handler Error." Besides preparing your dog, practice your handling technique, too.

## Besides, It Saves Postage

Here's a suggestion that may seem somewhat manipulative, though I see it rather as an exercise in common sense. If you're entering a trial with friends, mail the entries in one envelope. That increases the odds that your group's dogs will be placed next to one another during the Stays, instead of next to strange animals. Likewise, if there's bad blood between some of the dogs in your group, mail their entries several days apart. That lessens the chance that they'll be near each another during Stays.

## Double Commands

Exhibitors are permitted but a single command for each canine action. However, be aware that there's more than one type of multiple cue.

I once saw a gent nearly suffer a sputtering fit after challenging a judge over his score in a Novice ring. The judge informed him that he'd double commanded repeatedly during on- and off-leash heeling. The exhibitor claimed this was not so; that he'd commanded "Heel" only once whenever he moved his pet. The judge acknowledged that while it was true the gentleman gave but one verbal command with each initiation of heeling, it was equally true that every time he stopped he stamped his foot loudly, cuing the dog to Sit. Somewhat red-faced, the exhibitor shuffled away, muttering, and I mentally tipped my fedora to the judge for her integrity.

## Sermonette

I've been known to preach a bit to students who are soon to show. The sermon concerns the need for the group to help a member from getting down if things don't go right. A non-qualifying effort doesn't imply that dog or handler is a loser. They have merely gained valuable experience.

One who puts sincere effort into training and showing should not assume blame if things don't go well. Best is best, and it's difficult to condition for all that can occur at a show. By the same sign, a professional leaves the ring without sharing disappointments with his teammate. *Canis familiaris* isn't constituted to handle human emotional burdens. Negative vibrations only teach apprehension. When I overhear someone complain, "My dog let me down today," I feel sorry for the animal. No, I'm not suggesting that the dog understands the words, but I've no doubt he understands the tone. (It's also tempting to remind the person that it was he or she who trained the dog, obviously not too well.) Win, lose or draw, make sure pooch knows he's always your companion, and that he's ever Number One.

## Make a Check List

Before leaving for a show, make certain you have your entry confirmation, extra equipment (leash, collar, etc.), a first-aid kit, dog food, and drinking water—for pooch, not you. Changing water from city to city can produce a stubborn case of diarrhea. A capful of "RealLemon" in your pet's drinking water can be a helpful preventive, but it's still safer to bring water from home.

Another worthwhile caution is noting the name and telephone number of a local veterinarian near the trial site. The odds are you won't need the vet's services, but such preparation comes under the heading, "An ounce of prevention."

## When You Arrive

A method by which your pal can be eased into the commotion once you've arrived at a trial is to put his mind to rest, literally. At any show or trial, one can usually locate a more or less peaceful spot amid the confusion. Seat yourself at such a location, ostensibly ignoring all that's going on around you, and encourage your pet to stretch out for a nap. Given time, a temperamentally sound animal will lie down and very often will avail himself of the respite for a snooze.

After a while, gently wake your dog and take him from the site for a walk. If time permits, go for a short, relaxing drive. When you return, pooch will be more at ease than when you first arrived. This is because once a dog has been at a place, especially if he has slept there, he feels more at home the next time he's at the location, even if the occurrences are but moments apart.

## Thrice Around the Block

Don't warm up your dog by practicing at the trial. It's against the rules, and the sanctions can be harsh. Of course, you're allowed to heel your pet to the exhibition area—that's practical obedience—but drilling him at the site is forbidden. Too, such training is ineffectual. If pooch isn't ready by showtime, he won't be following a last-minute workout. Cramming only risks tiring and inhibiting your partner.

## To Cheat or Not to Cheat?

Forget it. A person might get away with this or that little trick in the ring, but it's nearly impossible to cheat one's way to a title. Besides, cheaters only deceive themselves. Sound training is not only easier, it's more productive.

## Ring-Wise

Have you ever heard the phrase "ring-wise"? It supposedly describes a dog who's been shown so many times at a specific competition level that he's learned the handler cannot, or will not, correct in a ring setting.

True, ring corrections are forbidden, but the ring-wise concept is a myth born of self-deception. It's a blame-the-dog defense that seeks to transfer responsibility for determining if an animal is ready for competition from handler to dog.

Granted, I've seen canines who've been unsuccessfully shown so many times that their behavior suggested they could probably go through the routine *sans* handler. But to say that a dog is ring-wise only begs the question. Rings don't teach; trainers do. In truth the animal has become *handler-wise*. He's learned that when the trainer "acts" in a certain way—nervous, irritable, rigid, tense, confused, apprehensive (it's a long list of possibilities)—he's no longer under that person's control. In a very real sense, the owner's behavior serves as something of a release cue. Moreover, it's the individual's behavior—not the dog's—that's being directly affected by the ring environment.

A canine who correlates human behavioral anomalies with being in a specific setting is one bright critter who probably should have earned titles long ago. The problem is the handler, and his or her change in manner when in a ring. The dog perceives the change and doesn't take the job at hand seriously.

### Ye Olde Match Trick

Fouling the ring or trial field is a disqualifier. While blame often centers on the dog, it bespeaks a major handler error. It's one matter for a canine to become ill or stressed in competition; it's another when he takes his routine 10:07 constitutional in the ring.

You can be relatively certain an accident won't occur by withholding food (but not water) the morning of competition, and by exercising and walking pooch prior to showing. If you feel he is holding it (stress can interfere with normal functions), a powerful stimulus can be a *paper* match. Just moisten the sulphur head with saliva, and gently insert the object where the sun doesn't shine. The match, etc., will be along shortly. The activated sulphur acts as just enough of an irritant to cause the desired result.

### Diplomacy Can't Hurt

Regardless of your performance, courtesy dictates thanking the judge before leaving the ring. If suggestions are offered, listen up, and be grateful for the extra time being spent. You may ask for comments, but judges aren't obligated to respond.

### Being Your Dog's Protector

While not wishing to induce paranoia, a matter to which you must attend with regard to dog shows is your pet's protection. There are those who have no compunction against taking things not belonging to them, your dog included. Never leave pooch unattended, even for a moment, nor ask a stranger to hold your leash while you attend to other business. I won't even allow strangers to pet my dog at a show. Before you decide that's overdoing it, realize that some sick people are lurking about. At a northern show some years ago, a stranger entreated a child to give a piece of meat "to the nice doggie over there." It was only alertness on the owner's part that prevented her pet from ingesting steak impregnated with tiny shards of glass.

Of course, such incidents are the exception rather than the rule. Most dog-show people are nice folks like you and me, if a trifle overzealous from time to time. The point is that all it takes is one nut-case to send you home with an indelible case of guilt. A little caution can forestall tragic memories.

## Reflection

> Don't fall into the trap of allowing yourself to become so engrossed in training and competition that you forget why you ever got a dog in the first place.
>
> Joel McMains

# 10

# Dog Problems and Problem Dogs

---

**Overview**

Though proper obedience training promotes desirable conduct, formal instruction isn't intended as a problem-behavior panacea. Heeling won't reform a digger, the Sit doesn't lessen excessive barking, the Finish can't stop car chasing. It's all very well for pooch to shine in class or competition, but that doesn't preclude his being a periodic holy terror around the house.

Obedience training's primary problem-behavior role is to provide a framework from which a trainer can operate. Training teaches a dog that the owner is a force to be reckoned with, that he or she has things to say, and the owner discovers how to communicate effectively with the dog.

**In General**

When problem behavior occurs, admonish the wrongdoer: "No!" or "Out!" according to the situation.* Use "No!" for things a dog should

---

*Exceptions to this rule are motion sickness and submissive urination.

never do (e.g., car chasing). "Out!" is for things you don't want pooch doing just then (e.g., barking). The rebuke alone may stop the problem, especially with a sound-sensitive animal or one who's learned not to challenge the leader's word. Don't punish long after the fact, though. That doesn't teach proper behavior: it teaches fear—of you.

## Excessive Barking

Periodic barking is normal. Your guardian's vocal warning is understandable, even desirable, when outsiders encroach upon his territory. Extended carrying on is another matter.

If a dog sees nothing to prevent him from doing what he wants, especially something as natural as barking, he does it. That's not mischief; it's being a dog. Accordingly, nothing short of an electronic bark-collar or surgery will universally deter barking when you aren't home. A less drastic option is to leave the animal in the house when you're away. That may not impede barking, but it mitigates the decibels your neighbors have to endure. When you're in residence, though, try the following techniques for silencing your budding opera star.

Since barking is often a product of boredom and unsatisfied needs, provide your pet something to chew. Hard objects, like (safe) animal bones and Nylabones, are preferable to soft articles—the latter don't last very long. No, don't appease with treats—that can worsen the problem. The moment your companion commences to yip and howl is not the time to rush to him with something gnawable. That rewards the behavior you're trying to stop. Just make sure he always has a chewy available. Two concepts operate here: first, a bone or similar article offers diversion. Second, a dog can't chew and bark simultaneously.

To teach your pet to hush when commanded, pursue the following. (This method is intended for outdoor dogs, as that's normally where a canine tends to warble. If your friend is usually indoors the task is easier as the animal is closer to hand.) One day when pooch commences to carry on in the yard, open the door, command, "Out," stare at the noisy one for a beat, and close the door. (Don't use "No," for two reasons: first, it's unrealistic to expect a dog never to bark. Second, at times you may want pooch to sound off, like when a stranger nears your home.) The surprise effect of your sudden appearance and curt announcement may cause a momentary lull, but likely no more than that. So far what we've done is create a starting point.

As the dog starts up again, walk purposefully to him, commanding (not yelling) "Out," with every step you take. The idea behind the "Out" litany is similar to that underlying the *verbal bridge* concept (see *Dog Logic*'s section on teaching Stays in chapter 8). It allows pooch to relate barking with that which is about to occur.

Seize the dog under the jaw area with one hand, and commence lightly cuffing his muzzle several times with the other, accompanying each open-handed blow with "Out." *The force of the blows should not be excessive.* The goal here is neither pain nor an exercise in dog-bashing—the objective is unrelenting pressure. Demonstrate that your response to being ignored won't end anytime soon. Again, the purpose is not to hurt the dog but to annoy him, in a manner similar to the annoyance that his barking creates. It's like a hornet buzzing about your head: the insect effects little more than an objectionable distraction, but you're aware of threatened additional grief.

Finally, mete out one final smack, shove the dog away, turn on your heel, and depart. Should you hear so much as a squeak during your exodus, spin around and go through the whole nine yards again. I know of a case where the procedure had to be used four times before the word penetrated. I've never heard of a fifth application being needed. One or two encounters generally convey the message.

Later, the next time you hear barking, appear in the doorway and command, "Out." As the dog pauses, praise, "Good Out, Good Out." That's the lesson's other half. Without this acknowledgement, a dog can't fully appreciate intent.

## Destructive Chewing

Cure this one through *replacement:* providing a Nylabone or the like so your pal can satisfy natural urges to chew without eating the house. Scold if you catch him chewing furniture, then pointedly communicate he should use a Nylabone. Don't reward with the bone—present it with an air of, "Chew this, not that!"

Should the problem persist, crate your pet when he can't be supervised (see "Housing and Housebreaking" in *Dog Logic*'s third chapter). Don't accompany crate-time with overtones of punishment, lest you impart negative attitudes about the nest. We're after prevention, not incarceration. The correct attitude is that you want pooch in the nest for reasons best known to yourself.

## Digging

The first curative for a dog with a fetish for digging the petunias is to remove him from viewing range, bury his stools in holes he's created, and cover them with an inch of soil. This approach can solve the canine-archeologist problem.

Should a more direct approach be needed, catch your pet in the act, after allowing him to create a deep hole. Next, fill said hole with water as he looks on. Then firmly dunk his muzzle in the water. *In no way do I imply you should risk drowning the dog;* you should keep his muzzle immersed for only a second or two. Then pull pooch out of the pond, shove him aside unceremoniously, and calmly fill the hole with dirt. Admonish, "No," once, while pointing toward the filled hole, and depart. You may have to repeat the sequence to make the point, but probably not twice.

## Jumping on You

Should your dog jump on you unbidden, the word "Off" accompanied by a knee to the chest generally does the job. In dealing with smaller canines, the *side* of your foot will have to do, but *not in the manner of a kick!* The objective is to brush the dog aside, not to risk injury. Increase force until you reach the degree of compulsion required to convince your pet you aren't funning with him.

With a large dog, another method is to grab the front feet as he jumps on you and thus keep him there for a few minutes. "You want to jump on me? Fine. You're staying awhile." Pooch may also have the opportunity to learn that he doesn't bite your hands, as dogs sometimes do when restrained in this manner. If he snaps, briefly release a foot, smack him openhanded in the chops simultaneous with "No" and grab the foot again. You don't need to knock the dog's head off—the idea is self-protection, not abuse—but the animal must be shown that snapping at you is wrong, today, tomorrow, and for all time.

Avoid disciplinary measures like stepping on back toes or sweeping your friend's back legs from under him. Yes, these approaches can teach, but the former risks snapping a toe and the latter can break a leg or dislocate a hip.

A related consideration is the lapdog who'd prefer to remain after being directed to depart. While a person can generally push off that size animal, a dog can misinterpret the action as rejection. It's better to teach that the word "Off" means you're going to stand in one second, regardless whether your companion is present. This is easily communicated by commanding, "Off," then standing (slowly, this first time), as though the animal weren't there. Don't follow "Off" with placing the dog on the floor. That teaches that "Off" means you're going to do the work of removing pooch from your lap. Better the animal should be shown that "Off" signifies *he* should do the work of removing himself from your lap. As he departs, praise, "Good Off."

## Jumping on Others

With problem behaviors it's often easier to teach a dog to do than to teach him not to do. Jumping on non-family members is one such instance. Instead of arguing with your pet whether he should be a nuisance (or, if he has the size, to knock someone flat), merely command, "Sit." "Sit" is a command you know how to enforce, and a sitting dog can't jump on anyone.

What a dog often discovers is *Alpha* can't or won't correct him around non-family members. Trainers sometimes don't follow through around strangers, especially "non-dog" people. Further, some dogs learn their trainers don't demand good behavior when someone is at the door. You must demonstrate that you not only can correct, but that you will. First, stage the situation. Arrange to have friends drop by, telling them to bear with you if the doorbell remains unanswered for a time. When the bell sounds, bring pooch near the door and command, "Sit—Stay," and head for the door. (It's helpful to have attached a collar tab earlier to provide a quick handle.) Command in a manner that conveys total confidence so that pooch will respond properly. If you show any hesitancy, the animal may sense uncertainly and try to exploit it.

If the dog doesn't respond by sitting firmly by the time you take your second step toward the door, return and correct him, momentarily ignoring the doorbell. Don't allow the animal to scoot even an inch after you've commanded, "Stay." Be alert for movement as you open the door, responding with appropriate force as needed. As the visitor enters, the dog may again try to move. Don't let him. As the caller enters and perhaps pets your friend, the animal must maintain the commanded position.

What's occurring, of course, is medium-stress distraction proofing. It's a contrived situation. The secret is that a dog can't realize this. For all he knows, you'll enforce your commands whether the person at the door is someone familiar or a total stranger. He doesn't know the difference, as the concept of another person being in cahoots with you to affect learning is beyond canine comprehension, at least in this situation.

## Getting into Garbage

The easiest solution is removing the garbage from your pet's access. If that's not possible, consider the following.

An old, yet effective remedy is placing mousetraps (*not* rat traps) atop the trash, covering them with a sheet of waxed paper (to increase their racket when triggered). After setting the stage, let nature take its course. Take no notice when the traps are sprung, so pooch doesn't associate the incident with you. Otherwise, the technique may only be effective when you're home.

Another method is adapting an avoidance technique similar to one used with seeing-eye dogs. When one of those animals allows the trainer to walk into an object, the person reacts by whaling the daylights *not* out of the dog, but out of the object. After witnessing a prolonged physical and vocal thrashing, sensitive canines pull away from such articles when next encountered. To apply this procedure to your trash-bucket invader, first place some tempting meat scraps in the receptacle. Do this without your dog present. Better he should discover them later, which he will. When pooch does find the tasties, suddenly appear and take the wastebasket to task, physically and verbally.

A third solution—one that isn't for the frail of spirit—is to use toilet tissue in a manner befitting the designer's intentions, then placing it in the trash pail, marking the container "Off-Limits." Odd types claim the technique is ineffective; it doesn't work. I hope they don't share their secret with my dogs and those of my students, as it certainly worked with them. It will with yours, too, if the animal sees you as *Alpha*. Pack underlings don't disturb areas *Numero Uno* has marked—it's that simple. If they do cross such lines, they haven't accepted you as pack leader.

## Getting on Furniture

Thwart this behavior by placing mousetraps (*not* rat traps) on the furniture or kitchen counter in question. The method has been around for a while, but that doesn't demean its effectiveness. Cover the traps with a few single sheets of newspaper—to hide them from view and to cause more noise when sprung. Ignore the event when pooch triggers one or more of the devices, as though you had nothing to do with it. Let the animal think the furniture bit him, so the lesson carries over when you aren't home. Gradually reduce the size of the newspapers until they— and the traps—have disappeared.

Don't do what one budding trainer did: forget the traps were there and proceed to repose on the guarded furniture. "It nearly gave me heart failure. Stung some, too."

## Problem Eating Habits

This habit—which ranges from eating fractional amounts to such quantities that obesity begins to undermine personality and threaten life span—is often inadvertently taught by well-meaning owners. Leaving food down constantly (known as *on-demand feeding*), or frequently changing brands, can breed poor eating habits. As dogs aren't fans of change, keep pooch's diet constant. Provide meals at two scheduled times daily. Remove the bowl after a set interval (ten minutes is normally ample for a dog to consume a meal), or when the animal is no longer interested in the repast.

Another condition that can induce erratic eating habits is allowing family members to annoy the dog during a meal. Just as you appreciate space at mealtimes, your pet likes peace and quiet then, too. Petting your companion as he's eating can have the same effect as teasing. Further, I've seen owners make their dog "Stay!" while the master prepares, fusses over and finally presents the bowl. Some intimidate the animal into holding the Stay awhile longer, especially if there are friends present to impress. A tactful scribe might term such treatment ill-advised. I call it mean and moronic. The last thing any animal needs during feeding is stress. Teaching pooch to balance a food bit on his nose briefly (at other than scheduled feeding times) until cued to toss and catch it is one thing. Interfering with his mealtime is churlish.

## Misdirected Anger/Housebreaking

This section's dual titling stems from the fact that owners often incorrectly perceive the phenomenon of misdirected anger as a housebreaking issue. This is because canine ire is typically expressed through fouling, though chewing furniture, raiding the garbage, and other similar acts are not uncommon.*

A German Shepherd Dog I owned years ago had a particularly nasty trait. When I'd go out for an evening, she'd not only soil the apartment, she once pulled clothing from a closet and made a deposit thereupon. Her

---

*Housebreaking is covered in *Dog Logic*'s third chapter. If you're training an older canine, substitute *dog* for *puppy*—the teaching principles for both are the same.

163

behavior was motivated by outrage at being left behind. Since I wasn't available to hear her complaints, she directed anger at things bearing my scent.

This occurred in the early 1960s, before airline cages were readily obtainable, and my living situation prevented me from keeping her outside when I was away. Today, given the proliferation of affordable airline crates, such problems should be approached via techniques outlined in *Dog Logic*'s third chapter, under "Housing and Housebreaking." An ensconced dog can't create soiling problems anywhere but there. Should the animal do so repeatedly, look for another dog. This unsavory type of canine mind-set—fouling the nest—is often symptomatic of genetically rooted attitudes that are difficult if not impossible to overcome reliably.

Understand: I'm not recommending that the dog who drops a load in the house be reflexively sent down the road. Such an occurrence is usually a housebreaking matter, and applying the method mentioned above corrects the difficulty in short order. I'm referencing the dog who *repeatedly* fouls his sleep area, his nest. That animal isn't sound, and while such inherent weaknesses can sometimes be acceptably modified, more often they can't.

A peripheral topic related to destructive behavior has more to do with owners than with their pets. I receive two or three monthly inquiries that follow a pattern. The caller tells me that upon returning home and finding that his pet had fouled, chewed, or otherwise violated the house, "Right away he knew he'd done wrong." I customarily ask, "Then why did the animal do what he did?" Nine times out of ten, the response is akin to, "Say what?", which clues me about the caller's lack of dog knowledge.

Without turning the subject into a needlessly complicated, psychological treatise, human discernment of canine guilt is often inaccurate. When finding that a dog has done some undesirable deed, an owner can mistakenly interpret the animal's manner as indicative of guilt. In fact, the dog is displaying anxiety in response to the owner's bearing. The animal has seen that glaring, tight-lipped stance before. Pooch isn't feeling guilt—he's scared. As the owner takes the dog to task, the animal crumbles further. The common result is internalized shame instead of positive learning.

A sad irony is that more often the fault lies with the owner than with his or her pet. Once the rules have been properly communicated to a sound canine, he won't violate them. That's basic to a pack animal's heritage. The educated dog who fouls the den during his owner's absence usually does so from an inability to "hold it," or from illness. A stable dog's method of managing his affairs doesn't entail subverting *Alpha*'s rules. It wouldn't occur to him to do so.

Events can produce cyclic owner ignorance. I know of a Labrador who was beaten mercilessly for tearing through a screen door. Though he'd never done anything similar before, his owner felt, "He should have known better." How a dog could possess such knowledge without prior learning is beyond me. The sum of any dog's information is his instincts (inherited knowledge) plus things he learns. As dogs aren't born with notions of good and evil with regard to storm doors, and given the owner's admission that the animal didn't have a history of destructive behavior, I concluded that the dog had better temperament than the owner.

What the Lab knew was that a bitch in heat was on the other side, and that he was driven to reach her. Yet, the owner maintained, "He still should have known better." I've often thought that were the world such that dogs picked their owners, some folks would never have canine companionship.

## Roaming

As I'm opposed to tying, Cruiser is best thwarted by a fence he can't defeat. No training guarantees arresting a dog's natural urge to roam, especially when other animals are near his yard, or when a female in season is in the area. An alternative is to keep pooch on-leash when outside. As Robin Roy, trainer at the Newington, Connecticut, K-9 Training Center, put it, "There's no foolproof way to keep a dog on your property. . . . you can't take the dog out of the dog."*

## Car Chasing

As with the rover, the only assured solution is a fence the dog can't overcome. If this isn't possible, enlist the aid of a friend with a car. Hide in the vehicle and direct a slow pass by your abode. As pooch rises to the occasion, your helper should brake promptly so you can quickly leap out and give the animal what for. With several helpers you can quickly

---

*Quoted by Carol Wyckoff in her article, "Country Roads and Dogs," in the Sept./Oct. 1990 issue of *Country Journal Magazine*, p. 60 (in the sidebar, "How to Keep a Dog at Home").

address the problem because you have many and differing vehicles from which to emerge unexpectedly.

## Misbehavior in a Vehicle

Some dogs who comport themselves civilly around the house seem to lose their minds during a car ride. Offenders often regard the family bus as their own private jungle gym and their owners as little more than annoyances. Further, an owner may have unintentionally taught through acquiescence that the dog may do as he wishes during trips. Now the critter must be shown that commands given in a vehicle carry the same weight as in any other setting.

The task is easier if you have access to a long driveway. If not, seek an infrequently traveled road. Be constantly alert for nearby traffic. You're going to be giving your brakes a workout, and an officer of the law (not to mention your insurance company) might be less than sympathetic to explanations that preoccupation with training your dog led to an accident.

Put your charge into the car, preferably in the backseat. Then, with your hands on the wheel but prior to starting the engine, command, "Platz." Watch pooch via the rearview mirror, as opposed to turning your head—he'll wonder how you knew what he was up to (or wasn't). If he complies, you don't have a problem at this stage. If he ignores the command, correct him.

Following any use of force, calmly relocate yourself behind the wheel, turn toward your dog, and summon him near the dividing seat. Pet him for a moment, then turn your back. The reason for calling pooch is to release him from the Platz so you can command him to lie down again momentarily. It's also to show that you haven't changed your mind that he's your pal; that disciplinary actions don't represent anything personal.

With exaggerated deliberateness, place your hands on the wheel and—in a normal tone—again command, "Platz." If pooch's head quickly sinks out of sight, dandy. That's the objective. If his response is sluggish, partial, or nonexistent, present an encore of the prior correction. Some dogs will need more than a single demonstration to get religion. I've yet to encounter one who required more than four. End the session after your student Platzes on command once.

The following day, repeat the scenario. If your dog Platzes as commanded, praise him and start the engine. Don't engage the gears yet, as the sound of the motor coming to life may cause the animal to get up.

166

Correct him if he does. Shift into gear with your foot on the brake. Should the resultant minor motion cause the animal to rise, shift out of gear and correct him. Quit the session by moving the car a few feet, parking it, and—if pooch remained Platzed—taking him from the area. If he didn't, repeat the series until he does. Don't end in failure.

The next session entails driving. With your pet in the back seat, command, "Platz." Praise as he complies. If no traffic is nearby, move the vehicle. When you can drive for fifty feet without a Stay violation, call it good for today.

Once you advance to driving along the previously mentioned, seldom-traveled road, command, "Platz," open a window or two as distractions (but not so wide that pooch could jump out), and motor along, ostensibly paying him no heed. When he maintains the Platz for a minute, stop, and call him near you. After some gentle petting, return to driving. Don't command, "Platz." Not yet. After you've driven fifty feet—and only after first making certain no traffic is nearby—command, "Platz," while the vehicle is moving. If the dog's head fails to drop like an anvil off a high building, immediately stop and correct him. Return to your driving. After a few moments, stop, summon your pet, visit with him momentarily, and repeat the sequence.

What we're attempting to revise is the dog's notion that you cannot or will not correct him when you're occupied with whatever it is you do when you're in that little room with the big window. That's about how your pet perceives the situation. What you must do is reeducate him that—while you can't ever take these steps on a four-lane expressway—he doesn't harbor the slightest doubt that you can, and that you will.

## Motion Sickness

This problem often has its origins in genetics, the smell of vehicular exhaust, prior stressful, vehicle-related experiences, or a combination of influences. Dramamine, an over-the-counter product, can help but is seldom a cure-all. (*Check with your veterinarian before using any form of medication!*)

The best long-term hope is *desensitization:* systematically lessening anxiety-producing responses through gradual exposure to increasingly stressful stimuli. Most owners can begin by putting pooch in the car, but I've outlined antecedent steps so not to shortchange those whose dog's problem is more ingrained. Regardless where you start, the dog shouldn't have been fed recently.

Should your companion display anxiety at any stage, remain there until he can handle the stress. As with any fear response, don't try to reassure the animal, either through petting or excessive verbalization. That often compounds the problem by rewarding undesirable behavior. The correct approach with a frightened canine is to seemingly overlook the response by directing your focus, and hopefully his, elsewhere.

Start by walking your pet near the vehicle. If he displays nervousness, the problem is likely chronic and you're in for extended conditioning. The near-term goal is being able to walk near the auto without provoking a fearful reaction.

The next phase is to walk your pet to the car, and open and close a door (but without either of you entering the vehicle). Should anxiety result, don't proceed until he's at ease at this stage.

Next, enter the vehicle and encourage your pet to join you. If he can't jump in due to size or nervousness, help him inside. Once there, pet him momentarily, then take him from the area.

The ensuing goal is for both of you to enter the car, and to start the engine. Let it run for only a moment, then remove your friend.

The next objective is to move the vehicle a few feet without inducing a negative reaction. The following day, drive slightly farther. Therapy now takes the form of longer excursions.

Reminder: Should you observe anxiety at any stage, immediately abort the session on as high a note as you can manage. Stay at that level until the animal is no longer discomfitted. The key to desensitization is increasing the pressure ever so slightly. Moving too quickly through the process can and usually does intensify the problem.

## Submissive Urination*

This one can be tricky. A dog often manifests the problem by piddling as he comes to you or during petting. While various authors counsel different approaches for modifying the behavior, they agree on one point: Discipline isn't the answer. Moreover, chastisement usually worsens the problem. Submissive urination can be the product of genetics, environment, or both. It often indicates a dog overly sensitive to sound and/or motion. Thus, force or harsh verbal abuse can deepen the problem. Similarly, reassurance like "Oh, poor baby!" rewards and perpetuates the behavior as it constitutes praise in a non-praise situation.

---

*A case study is presented in *Dog Logic*'s chapter 14, "Lessons From the Best Teacher," under "But the Pitifulness of Myself . . ."

There's a requirement for using my method of alleviating the condition: The dog has to crave being petted. Fortunately, most submissive wetters do. The curative is simple, but as mentioned, it's tricky—timing is everything. You have to teach your pal you won't pet him when he's dribbling or is about to. Consider these examples.

You reach to pet your dog, and he responds by squatting or piddling. Immediately shift your gaze to the rear of his anatomy, say "No, no," withdraw your hand and walk away.

Your pet comes to you and either assumes the position or is wetting during the approach. Immediately shift your gaze to the rear of his anatomy, say "No, no," and walk away.

Your pet comes to you, or you reach to pet him, and he responds by rolling onto his back. Immediately shift your gaze to the rear of his anatomy, say "No, no," withdraw your hand, and walk away. True, in this case the animal hadn't started to urinate, but with a *submissive* piddler, it's better to pet only when he's in the on-his-paws position, at least until the problem clears. To do otherwise is to reward submission, and that's unwise because the posture is only one step from urination.

When telling your pet, "No, no," keep the tone light and conversational, as opposed to one of "barking" commands. The animal could interpret gruffness as pressure. As mentioned in the first paragraph, any form of harshness can only work against you in dealing with this problem.

Don't expect results overnight. The curative process can take several weeks. Just make up your mind there are certain behaviors you won't accept—piddling, squatting, rolling over, even a lowered head. You simply won't pet pooch under any of those conditions. You'll reward confidence, but not fear.

## Aggression toward Humans

This section's purpose is to help trainers protect themselves against the buzz-saw effect a dog on the fight can create. Though fighters are rare, they do exist, and a person can find him- or herself suddenly and seriously threatened with little or no warning or preamble. Despite a person's best-intended overtures, some dogs physically rebel against domination, even to the extent of tentative or outright aggression. Should this occur you have three options. One, part company with the animal. Two, deflect the critter's actions, hoping he'll quickly see the folly of his ways. Three, meet the challenge head-on with appropriate and uncompromising retaliation. Selection of one over the other is a matter of trainer temperament, capability, knowledge, experience and judgment, coupled with his or her reading of the dog.

In most cases I initially opt for the deflection path, for three reasons. First, it normally dissuades a dog from his ill-fated course without any obvious effort on my part. This serves to enhance my status in his eyes, as the animal finds his aggression thwarted through relatively peaceful means. Second, deflection requires only good reflexes, timing and moderate agility. Confrontation often requires a good deal of strength and leverage in addition to those attributes. Last, if a physical clash between us is inevitable, I would greatly prefer that it occur at a time and place of my choosing, not the dog's.

Should your pet display aggression toward you or any family member, and if you've the slightest inkling the animal might be more than you can safely handle, stop right there. Back off, isolate him, and seek professional help. *Don't* confront the dog. Human anger, fear, and a feeling akin to indignant outrage can combine to drive a person into battle, but don't succumb to such emotions. Canine contacts with the world of swift and all-out violence are more recent than ours. He may be far more skilled at it than you.

If you chose the first option—sending the animal on his way—you can do so with the dog in one of two states: alive, or otherwise. Finding a home for a troublesome canine can be difficult, but the effort can later reward you with the knowledge that you didn't overreact by putting away a pooch who might have had a good life in a different situation. An example of this is the puppy a person acquires, only to discover months later that the little one has grown into a small horse who's developed the habit of occasionally raising a lip toward his people. The odds are this dog might not be a problem in other hands; the owner simply wound up with more than he or she bargained for. That doesn't imply anything is "wrong" with dog or person. It only suggests a mismatched relationship.

Should you decide the dog must go, and if you feel that he might do well in a home more suited to his size, strength and temperament, you can pursue several routes. Advise veterinarians of your intent. They receive many inquiries from people looking for dogs. Inform the local animal shelter. Contact breeders and trainers. Run a classified ad, and make announcements on local radio station's public-service programs.

If you feel that you and the general public would be better served by having the dog dispatched, seek professional counsel before taking this irreversible step. Obviously, there's no going back. In some sad cases, the adorable if somewhat frantic and feisty (or fearful and withdrawn) pup you bought for the kids last Christmas develops into a legitimate threat to those children, as well as to you and your spouse. Moreover, you can discover by visiting with your veterinarian and/or experienced dog people that there are no good solutions for dealing with some animals. In such an admittedly tragic case, let him go before he injures someone. It can be a difficult step to take, but a lamentable fact is that some dogs aren't "right" for any situation. Through no fault of yours or theirs, they're walking time-bombs, and as such are better put down.

If you ever find yourself in such a troubling situation, I caution you against swearing off dogs for all time. It's a natural defense against risking further pain, but I hope you can see the irrationality of such a decision. Just as it's unfair to judge other dogs against the memories of Old Buster (see *Dog Logic*'s second chapter), it's equally unwise to take the pledge because of an opposite experience. A person could unknowingly rob him- or herself of many joyous moments.

Now consider the animal who is neither beyond salvation nor incapable of being handled safely. Since I've not met your dog, telling you to do this, that, and the other thing if attacked is imprudent. How I recommend responding to aggression from an adolescent, female Chow Chow, for instance, is different from the approach I'd take with an adult, male Rottweiler. So instead of offering a list of "Foolproof Steps To Take if Beset," and possibly causing you or yours injury, I offer a generic, first-person-singular scenario of *my* response to being attacked—not merely menaced—by a large, powerful dog who is obviously bent on *my* serious harm.

**Be warned that the following is more than risky, it's *highly dangerous*.** It's never easy, and most people have no business trying to contend with canine aggression. It is always unsafe, as a dog can overpower most humans with surprising ease. Do it often enough (once can be all it takes) and you'll lose. Injury is scant inches away, and a person doesn't have to err by much to be severely hurt or maimed. I have to take on such animals; *you don't!*

Should a dog wheel and charge, I wait until the last second and pivot away on either foot. This causes the animal to sail by, thereby deflecting his intention.

Admittedly, this maneuver cannot be performed by everyone. It requires agility and good timing. Successfully thwarting a canine attack requires such skills, though, regardless of the preferred method. That's partly why *Dog Logic* cautions that a person shouldn't work a dog he or she can't physically handle when the heat's on.

My next tack is to immediately command, "Sit," to initiate control. An aggressive dog who's had some training often reacts properly out of sheer habit. Should he not respond, I'd correct for failure to Sit (using minimum force, so not to incite his fire anew), thus shifting the basis for contention from aggression to disobedience. Assuming he does Sit, the next command is "Stay," to allow us time to settle.

If the animal initiates a second advance, deflection would be abandoned forthwith in favor of knocking him into next week, as it were. If that characterization seems harsh, I suggest that so is being the object of forty-two teeth with several hundred pounds of jaw pressure behind them. Habitual aggression can't be tolerated, and if a dog commits the cardinal sin of repeated snapping, he must be firmly confronted—that's the nature of his world. (Remember from *Dog Logic*'s first chapter, one must train at the *dog's* level of understanding.) Halfway measures are both improper and ineffective once a fight is joined. Humans aren't puncture proof, and should any dog persist in bringing push to shove, you're obligated to respond such that he will cease and desist, now and for all time.

The rule in such occurrences is go to the dog—don't back away. Retreat can draw him to you with heightened confidence. Going toward the animal makes a dual statement: One, you can handle him; two, some things are always wrong, and snapping at you is most assuredly one of those things.

Finding myself assaulted, I leash-jerk the dog onto his back legs (but not off the ground), wrapping excess lead around the muzzle. I flip pooch onto his back, straddle him, and pin his throat by grabbing fur and skin over the windpipe (but not the airway itself), while *openhandedly* smacking (don't use a fist) the daylights out of his muzzle with the other hand. My firm if not loudly voiced, broken-record litany is, "No! No! No! Don't you ever even think it!" I put my face as close to his beak as I dare (while keeping at least one hand on his throat), make eye contact, and advise him in the calmest, meanest, dirtiest voice I own, "The last dog who tried that shtick is buried right over yonder, and you're about to join him!" It's not true, of course, but the beast who endangers my welfare must be responded to in kind if he's to learn. Also, the words help me generate intensity to impart clear meaning.

In this manner of discipline—pinning a dog—the handler risks his or her back and sides being scratched by the animal's rear legs. Such injury beats being bitten, though, and the technique places the handler in a position of total domination and the dog in one of complete submission. The procedure's effectiveness is such that I recall only two dogs I had to pin twice. Once was sufficient for the few others I've had to flatten.

I then stand slowly, taking care to protect myself, command, "Fuss" (to perpetuate control), and hope for better days. If the dog reattacks, we are again going to the ground, only this time I squeeze off the beast's wind momentarily. I'm no fan of this defensive technique, but neither am I fond of emergency-room visits, shots and stitches, especially when they're mine.

Once the smoke clears, one of the more difficult things to do is one of the more necessary: I offer the animal my hand. The dog may sniff, lick, or ignore the hand, but he may not growl or snap. I present it directly in front of and a few inches from his nose, keeping thumb in and fingers slightly curled, instead of protruding invitingly. It's easier to sense a bite coming when the hand is positioned thus: a dog has to move more of his body, slowing him somewhat and affording me more reaction time. Placing it to the side of the muzzle is riskier since that provides him a quickness advantage: to bite he need only turn his head. If he responds acceptably, I pet him and we get back to work. Should he react aggressively, I show him via an encore of the foregoing that hell hath no fury like a trainer scorned.

Now, please understand three points, and understand them well. First, the foregoing characterizations of reacting to an attacking dog are undeniably violent. They may even seem brutal. But remember that the dog I am referring to is a statistical anomaly: an animal who is not just snarling and otherwise skirting the edges of aggression, but one with blood in his eye who is trying his level best to take me out. If his force cannot be deflected, it must be met and overcome by a greater force or the dog will be victorious. Trying to placate such an animal can result in a trainer being not just nipped but maimed. Second, in the final analysis I am trying to do the dog the ultimate favor. If I didn't care about him, I would just say, "To hell with it," call the owner, and let him or her put the animal away. In confronting the dog—in trying to teach him "Thou shalt not!"—I am trying to keep him alive. More than once I have seen my actions help a problem dog turn a corner, from an "If you can't settle him we're going to have to put him to sleep" dog into a more than acceptable companion. The animal simply had to be shown in a way he could understand that he was not destined to be pack leader. Third, I restate an earlier warning: If you've the slightest inkling the animal might be more than you can safely handle, stop right there. Back off, isolate him, and seek professional help. *Don't* confront the dog.

So far the topic of canine aggression toward humans has focused on hostility toward family members generally and the trainer specifically. Still, some dogs habitually fire at nonthreatening strangers, a condition that has its origins in weak genetics, faulty learning or both. As no foolproof panacea exists for this problem, always keep such a dog on-leash when around people. Second, when unreasonable aggression occurs, swat the animal openhanded under the chin and admonish, "Out." (Take care this doesn't cause the animal to turn on you.) Third, and perhaps most important, *don't* attempt to settle pooch through reassurance and petting. This is the error I see most often. The practice rewards for the very behavior you're trying to stop—the dog is being praised for doing the wrong thing.

### Fighting with Other Dogs

The primary rule during a dogfight is to first, last, and always protect yourself. Intrusion can cause one or more of the animals to turn reflexively on you. Putting one's hands into the fracas can be not unlike thrusting them into a threshing machine. Using feet is somewhat safer, but not to any great degree. Don't waste lung power yelling at the combatants—they probably won't hear you. Even if they do, the odds are your verbalized emotions will only spur them on.

The first order of business with any canine altercation is to get it stopped. A long-handled broom can be effective when the bristles are jammed into the dominant animal's nostrils. A mild-voltage shock-stick can also be useful, especially when applied to a flank. Water from a hose can halt the proceedings, but take care not to shoot a forceful stream into an eye.

Once the melee is terminated, my practice is to take each animal by under-neck fur (assuming the battle was between two dogs only), and—with them facing me—bring their heads together smartly (but not with sufficient force to risk injury). I then advise them in the most controlled yet threatening voice I can muster that should they wish to fight in the future, they can start with me. (I accompany this admonition with a silent prayer that neither takes me up on the offer.) My messages are *I* am pack leader, and *I* do not tolerate such contests among underlings. I thus separated my male German Shepherd Dog from my male Doberman the single time they got into it, and to date an encore hasn't been needed (for which I am ever thankful).

A little common sense can go a long way toward a peaceful situation, too. If you have several dogs and know that bad blood exists between certain of them, either keep them separate or reduce the pack size.

Some *Canis familiaris* members are more canine-aggressive than others. Such animals may be disinclined toward raising a lip toward a human or the family feline, but often display hostility toward other dogs. This tendency is often gender related: males antagonistic toward males, females resentful of females. This trait gives rise to expressions such as "dog-aggressive," "male-aggressive," etc. Other factors often elemental to the equation are heightened senses of territory and/or dominance.

One final thought: Children have no business trying to stop a dogfight. Make certain that your youngsters know this as well as they do not to play in traffic. That either can result in serious injury—or even be fatal—is no exaggeration.

## The Chicken Killer

An effective, timeworn approach is tying a deceased chicken around the culprit's neck such that he can neither dislodge nor chew it. Tradition has it that the bird remains affixed for two to four days, or as one wag put it, "Until the fowl is truly foul." The idea is that a canine thus encumbered develops a pronounced aversion to a bird's presence.

An alternate method involves tying a chicken by one foot to a post, and attaching a wire from a fence charger to the other leg's yellow area. Attaching the wire thus allows current to be conducted, but the creature doesn't feel it. The bird must be on a surface that prevents it from being grounded, but which is small enough that a dog can't place all four feet upon it. Otherwise, he won't receive a shock either.

Once all is in readiness, let your pet out and allow nature to take its course. Whatever his reaction when the juice bites, ignore it. Better you shouldn't even be in the area. The dog mustn't relate your presence with the event or the lesson may be effective only when you're nearby.

## Reflection

*The truth I do not stretch or shove*
*When I state the dog is full of love.*
*I've also proved by actual test,*
*A wet dog is the lovingest.*

Ogden Nash

# 11

# Lessons from the Best Teacher (Part II)

---

**T**HE CLOSING CHAPTER of *Dog Logic* presents training anecdotes intended to deepen understanding and appreciation of our best friend, what drives him, and of the human-canine relationship. The theme continues here, with incidents providing less-than-incidental information.

## Counterproductive Messages

The caller wanted her Doberman to cease and desist trying to take on the world. The problem had reached the point that whenever she took the year-and-a-half-old male for a walk, a stranger approaching within fifty feet elicited barking, bared teeth and straining at the leash. People knocking at the owner's door were unknowingly taking their lives in their hands.

"Jack began acting like this when he was five or six months old, and he's gotten steadily worse since."

Surmising the problem's origin, I suggested that she and her companion stop by my kennels to see what might be done.

A few days later she and pooch arrived. As I approached them the Doberman came unglued, growling, snapping and lunging toward me.

As I had suspected might be the owner's reaction, the lady reflexively attempted to calm the animal with petting and, "It's all right, Jack, it's all right." I asked that she put the dog in her vehicle so we might discuss the situation.

What was operating, of course, was basic protection-training reinforcement. Months ago the then puppy had tentatively gurgled at a stranger, the owner communicated unintended approval via petting and non-negative verbalization, and the reinforcement cycle was begun. True, the intent was to pacify the dog, to settle him, but just the reverse was the effect. Essentially, the owner was praising the Doberman for the very behavior she wanted stopped. It's what I do when training a guard dog who properly shows aggression toward an agitator (bad guy). My praise tells the animal, "That's right, pooch, that's right!"

It's a typical mistake, commonly occurring when the training of dogs is consciously or subconsciously likened to the rearing of children. Reassurance can be helpful with an out-of-control child, but the same technique applied to a fired-up dog usually exacerbates the difficulty.

The first order of business was educating the owner, and the first lesson was that eradication of the problem was out of the question. Lurking in the recesses of Jack's doggy mind will always be vague impressions of what he used to do and how he used to react, especially in high-stress situations, which often act as triggers. A dog never forgets, and with Jack having had more than a year of conditioning, behavior modification was the best that could be hoped for.

To that end, I suggested that the animal be taken through my basic obedience class. The goals were to establish the owner as *Alpha,* teach her about canine nature while providing on-leash control, and show the dog that he could exist around unfamiliar humans without aggression. Over time the Doberman settled markedly, due in part to the effects of conditioning *vis-à-vis* the class settings, and to the owner's rightful assumption of the leadership role, which took much of the inciting pressure from the dog's shoulders. He no longer had to make the decision to fire as it was no longer his to make. Of course, that's much of what had led to the problem in the first place. Through no fault of his, the dog had been put in a position of calling the shots. Now, when a situation precipitates that old feeling, he looks to the owner for direction and accedes to her wishes.

### "Warm as Toast, Thank You"

It was one of those Wyoming winters that made me long for the Southlands. High winds, massive snowfalls, extensive drifting and record wind-chill readings. One December night as the mercury fluttered to 39 below, Murphy's Law held sway—the power went out. No lights, and more important, no heat. Though electricity was restored several hours later, things got a little dicey in the interim. The house is well-insulated, but with the howl effecting a wind chill I don't even want to think about, inside temperature dropped rapidly. What does this tale of woe have to do with a canine-training book? Read further.

We share a great deal with our pets, and in many ways: companionship, working, hunting, competition—it's a long list. That particular night, my German Shepherd Dogs—Smokey and Marty—and I shared heat. I stretched out on the living room carpet near the wood-burning stove, commanded them to Platz on each side of me, pulled blankets over the three of us and gave thanks.

Doubtless I would have survived without the dogs' 101 degrees' contribution—I was wearing so many sweaters and coats that I looked like a walking Michelin ad. But along with sharing body heat, we also shared another very special kind of warmth.

If anyone ever asks you how training and bonding interrelate, mention this vignette. Without both, the Shepherd Dogs would not have remained the night. Obedience got them onto the floor, bonding kept them there.

### Perfectionism's Price

Clancy was a two-year-old male Great Pyrenees. His owner had taken the animal through my novice class and was preparing for AKC Novice competition. A natural trainer, he learned rapidly, until a fatal flaw finally caught up with him: He was one of those folks who wouldn't be satisfied if he were hung with a new rope.

Though their size may seem to belie the fact, Pyrs are sensitive. Approval means as much to them as to any breed. They can handle censure but not injustice. One day during a practice, as Clancy executed an exuberant Flip Finish, an errant front paw touched the handler. Before I could move, the man severely blasted the dog for the minuscule error. That was the last time Clancy ever did a Flip for his owner.

Over the ensuing weeks the animal's overall working attitude went down and stayed down. In a phrase, he lost his edge. Moreover, it was stolen from him. Knowing that the owner aspired to competition honors, I appealed to his motivation by pointing out that canine self-esteem often goes hand in hand with top scores; that unintentional goofs should be ignored; that Clancy should be praised for his desire, but I might just as well have been talking to myself.

When a trainer demands continual perfection, he or she risks losing far more than can ever be regained. Often driven by all the wrong reasons, such an owner corners his companion into an impossible position. Once a dog senses hopelessness—of pleasing *Alpha,* in this case—a good part of the animal shuts down.

Footnote: Things sometimes work out. It seems that business setbacks led his owner to sell Clancy, and the dog wound up in a home where he was loved for what he was, instead of exploited for what he could do. Clancy is doing Flip Finishes again.

### Gotcha!

Perhaps you're familiar with the *fear-biter* concept. It refers to a dog who arrives at the *fight or flight* state with no more provocation than occurs during normal contact situations. Petting can set him off.

Though fear biters are rare, an even scarcer mutant is the *sneak biter.* Like the fear biter, this animal's behavior isn't a product of his own making. It's genetically based. The dog has no control over it. Unlike the fear biter, the sneak won't nail a person out of fright—this pooch's motivator is pure cussedness. He enjoys setting up trust in an individual, and once he has you in that state, "Gotcha!"

The last dog of this persuasion I encountered was a Dingo, whom I met at a seminar some years ago. The animal was giving his owner a hard time, refusing to do lessons he'd supposedly mastered months earlier, and it was obvious the handler needed to be firmer. Jake was one tough critter, and as you know from *Dog Logic,* a trainer must be one inch tougher than the animal (but no more than that), or the dog trains the person. Do not confuse this dog with the dog who feels threatened—very rare.

I took the leash, swapped the choker for a small pinch collar, and commenced healing. The Dingo gave me some static, but a couple of firm corrections conveyed the message that I wasn't funning with him.

Confrontation of prolonged resistance often leads a dog to momentarily display a case of the sulks, but this animal's attitude actually started to come up. While that's not a definitive sign—some dogs revel in suddenly discovering they no longer have to maintain the *Alpha* role— such behavior from this particular dog was a clue that eluded me.

I paid for the lapse. I'll have the scars the day they put me in the ground. Following an Automatic Sit, the Dingo jumped toward me three times in happy-dog fashion. Something kept me from bending to praise the animal—that's how I normally respond to such fire—and I thank God my sixth sense was operating or the animal might have gotten me in the face. As it was, after hypnotizing me with his three happy-dog, "Gee-I-like-you!" leaps, in the split second it took him to turn his head during the fourth, his whole manner changed. His eyes took on a crazed look. In that instant I identified him, saw what was coming, and knew I was out of time. The dog took me just above the kneecap. He didn't nip, mind you—he sank his teeth in as far as they'd go. And hung on.

Pressure on a nerve near the rear of his jaw got the dog off me, and—to my credit—I didn't knock him through the nearest wall. It was tempting to respond as though the word "football" was stenciled on the animal, but I realized that the incident was past as far as the dog was concerned. Belatedly recognizing him for what he was, I knew hostility from me would be pointless; it wouldn't accomplish anything. Landing on this type of dog won't show him the folly of his ways—it'll only motivate him to start planning the next attack. I settled for commanding, "Sit," handed the leash to his owner, and tottered off in search of hydrogen peroxide.

Temper almost did get the better of me moments later. That was when the dog's owner informed one and all, "Yass, he's nailed everyone in the family at least a couple of times." It was information I'd like to have had prior to working the dog. Bad-tempered canines are one thing, but less-than-candid owners are another.

As a highly respected trainer once told me, though, "You get bit, that's part of it, too." She's right. It comes with the job. I'm fortunate to have been severely bitten only twice since 1975. I'm equally blessed that those isolated incidents haven't made me paranoid around new dogs. Confidence is integral to training—you have to be able to radiate trust to have a chance of receiving it. I've learned much over the years about reading canine intent, but even so, I don't know that I'd see another sneak biter's plan unfolding in time to prevent injury.

So, what to do with a dog like this? First, realize that no one is going to "fix" him. Colloquially, he's tetched. With behavior dictated by forces beyond his control, he has no choice in being the way he is. The animal can't be changed to a degree that one could guarantee that he'd never be a threat again. He's one step from being full-time vicious, and is unable to learn from the consequences of his actions. A dog who draws a person in with contrived displays of affection and enjoyment, and then savagely bites when the individual buys the act, should be put away before he maims someone. I don't relish telling an owner that his or her pet should be put down—it's a part of the business that I'll never enjoy—but in an obvious case like this, I'd rather be straight with a someone than keep my silence and later learn that the dog took off someone's fingers, or worse.

## E.S.P?

Does a lavish turkey dinner have a sedating effect on you like it does on me? I customarily partake of my Thanksgiving bird-and-trimmings feast around two in the afternoon, and by three I'm usually looking for a place to sack out.

The problem with sleep and a full stomach is the digestive action can induce less-than-restful dreams. One Thanksgiving I dreamed I was in a shabby neighborhood in a large city. It seemed to be about 3:00 A.M., and hoodlums were menacingly advancing toward me. I thought repeatedly, "I wish Smokey were here," Smokey being my German Shepherd Dog and as good a canine friend as I've ever been so fortunate to have. The next thing I knew, Smokey was licking my face, bringing me to the surface. Further, he was a heartbeat from firing, as though he perceived trouble nearby and was seeking direction from me: "Just show me where they are."

Had I called out in my sleep? No. I'd failed to switch off a bedside tape machine I'd activated to record some notes for *Dog Logic*. It was still running, and a playing of the tape revealed no sound. A friend here for the holiday related that Smokey had been sleeping by the fireplace and had suddenly bolted to the bedroom for no apparent reason.

Have I witnessed similar experiences, when a dog seemed to read a human's mind? I could fill a book with such memories. E.S.P.? I suppose that's an adequate label for the phenomenon. Spooky? Not at all. No more so than any other natural occurrence. Is your dog capable of such communication? Of course. It's part of him. As mentioned in *Dog Logic*'s fifth chapter, "In a very real sense, your pet hears your inner voice." Constantly.

## So You Want to Be a Trainer

In seeking my niche I've worked as a radio announcer and copywriter, a performing musician and teacher, an accountant, a hotel manager, a cop and a software instructor. I enjoyed each job, but none provided the satisfaction I derive from working with dogs. To those who aspire to train professionally, though, I'd be less than candid were I to infer that the vocation is a perpetual bed of roses. Consider the case of Sniff, a German Shorthaired Pointer I trained some years ago.

When the eight-month-old dog and his owner arrived, the gulf between them was profound. The animal wasn't merely indifferent to human presence, he didn't seem to know that anyone else was on the planet. The "Why?" was obvious: To his owner, Sniff was just another "thing" in an arsenal of ego gratifiers—the chauffeured, mega-bucks car, the forty-four-inch television, the purebred, registered hunting dog. The phrase "emotionally starved" ran through my mind. The degree to which the pup was seeking family ties became more evident during our first few sessions. Sniff bonded to me as quickly as any dog I've known.

The program's twenty eight days flew by. The Pointer learned rapidly and well, and his zest for life increased exponentially. Finally came the day for the owner to reclaim him. I delivered a lengthy discourse about the need for contact and bonding between man and dog, and I like to think that some of it took. I can only hope it did. But if I live to be ninety-nine I'll never forget the way Sniff's spirit seemed to shrivel as he put two and two together, looking from me to the owner and back to me when they were reunited, and how the heartsick animal stared in quiet dignity at me from the car's back window until they were out of sight.

Would-be professional trainers: Know what you're letting yourselves in for. It can be a most gratifying vocation, but there are times when things can really get under your skin. I know: you can't live for the dog, and you can't own them all, and no one can give them a home like you can. Intellectually you know all that. Still, there are times when an event can cause you to mutter to yourself for weeks.

## Jiggs

The foregoing demonstrates an undesirable facet of training professionally. But time paints happy pictures in memory, too.

Jiggs was a two-year-old Blue Heeler who snapped at ankles. His owner had ingrained the habit via puppyhood lessons to bite at her foot. She'd tied cloth around her ankle, and showed the pup what fun it was to snap at the material as she walked. "It was a cute thing to teach a *Heeler*, don't you see? I figured he'd grow out of it as he got older." Some people . . .

Anyway, the owner's boyfriend had assured her, "*I'll* break the dog of that!" Machoism, combined with zero knowledge, a five-watt mentality, and a low boiling point, had resulted in a very toughened dog who still liked to snap at ankles, but who now was additionally terrified of men. "My boyfriend says we ought to shoot my dog. Can you fix him?"

Uncertain who was meant by "him," I remember thinking I'd likely reach the Heeler, but that the boyfriend was probably a lost cause. Seeing the trembling animal turn his head away as I approached (which I call the *ostrich defense*) made me surer of both conclusions.

Have you ever seen or heard a dog's teeth chatter in fear? It's a stress reaction that I've witnessed on mercifully few occasions. Excessive salivation often accompanies the reaction, as do rapid, shallow breathing and jerky, shuddering blinking. That was Jiggs's response, along with leaning away from me as I touched him. I hurriedly secured the owner's signature on my training contract, and got her down the road before she could change her mind.

When you train for a living you take some dogs knowing that inordinate time and effort will be needed. You accept that because you know that you're probably the only chance the animal's got. That's known philosophically as giving something back, and in the case of Jiggs, the owner had made it plain that if she struck out here, the next—and last—stop would be with the boyfriend and a shotgun at the county landfill.

You may recall from *Dog Logic* that I normally allow a dog a few days of settling-in time before commencing training. With Jiggs, I started right after the owner departed. Not on heeling, sits, and so forth—secondary material could wait. Contact, however, had to begin right away. Had I left him to his own devices for a time, Jiggs might have withdrawn to an unreachable point.

The frightened animal followed me on-leash to the training yard. Along with the ostrich defense, this was further evidence of learned helplessness—he'd lost his will to resist that which scared him. After seating myself near the base of an old ash tree, I leaned comfortably against it and began a silent meditation technique I use to unwind. The animal's pitiful state had churned my emotions, and I needed to release my tension or Jiggs would sense it and contact would be blocked.

When the moment was right, I began to talk to pooch in the softest, gentlest voice I possess. Commenting on everything from weather to what a fine dog he was, I periodically canted my head to one side and then to the other, the way a dog does when he's trying to understand something. After a few minutes Jiggs looked at my eyes. That's when I shut up and began softly patting my leg. He must have seen something he liked because he tried to come to me. Three or four times he flinched in my direction, but he couldn't seem to send the message to his legs. His upper body jerked toward me, but his feet remained rooted. It wasn't a neurological problem—the dog had learned fear to a paralyzing depth. I gave a very light, beckoning tug on the leash, and Jiggs started to walk-stumble toward me. His head was down, and only the tip of his drooping tail wagged, but even so it was a joyous moment: his desire for contact was overriding his fear. As the dog sniffed my outstretched, palm-up hand, I began to caress the underside of his jaw. I pulled my hand back a millimeter at a time, bringing him closer as he followed it. Finally, he was alongside my leg, and I was soon able to get him to lie down, leaning against me. After a few minutes, lulled by gentle petting, he drifted into a state. It wasn't sleep, really—more one of semi-consciousness, akin to a trance. Periodically a leg jerked, and his eyes popped wide open, slowly closing after a few seconds of wide-eyed staring. Knowing that whatever level of relaxation Jiggs reached that day was induced by exhaustion and a feeling of relative safety, the phrase "nervous wreck" passed through my mind.

Our next few "training sessions" were similar to the first one: walks around the training yard, visiting, petting, contact. And a new name. "Jiggs" was a sound the dog associated with bad times, so "Jiggs" became "Sammy."

Once Sammy and I started the obedience phase of his time here, it became obvious that this was a dog who wanted to please. He learned quickly, responding to praise with a "Look at me—I did it right!" attitude of fulfillment. As the pooch had yet to snap at my ankles, I decided to elicit the behavior so it could be addressed.

First I donned scratch pants (leather leggings designed to prevent injury during guard-dog training). Then I sporadically moved my feet with enticing suddenness during heeling. Finally Sammy obliged me by taking a shot at my left ankle. I stopped (to draw attention to the moment), stared at him briefly, said, "No—(*pause*)—Fuss," and commenced heeling again. I continued to occasionally move my feet in tempting manner, and as I saw Sammy thinking about nipping and deciding not to, I praised, "Good Fuss, Good fuss," affirming that he was doing the right thing by ignoring the urge to bite.

Snapping at ankles had developed into a play activity in his mind. That's what his owner had unintentionally taught by shifting the accent from primal herding instincts to play drive. Had she not done so, stopping the behavior would have been much more difficult. The boyfriend, in trying to beat the game out of the dog, had only infused a "Try harder!" attitude. The animal had learned that the beatings were intended to make him fight to play the game. Were this not so, my one "No—Fuss" (i.e., "Fuss" means "Heel without biting") wouldn't have sent the message. Approval, which the dog had been fervently seeking all along, cemented the no-biting lesson.

I alluded to a rewarding finale to this tale. You've yet to read it. Yes, Sam was able to shed his cocoon of fear. And yes, he quit snapping at ankles and developed into a very well-trained dog. Those facts alone are great news. But the best part concerns his owner and her boyfriend: Happily, I never saw or heard from them again. Ma Bell's recording informed me their phone had been disconnected, and the owner of the trailer they were renting advised that they'd left without paying some back rent.

After the required folderol of placing advertisements and securing a small-claims court judgement, I made a few telephone calls. Today, Sammy has a super home on a Montana ranch. Every year a special Christmas card arrives. With it is a picture of Sammy, and I reflect that I'm in a pretty rewarding business.


## Don't Blink!

Fred and I had attended college together. A frequent summer visitor to my home, he's a good person, not given to unkind comments about mankind (save for the occasional scathing remark about politicians), but when it comes to how to comport oneself around canines, Fred needs direction. Knowing that, I mentioned during his first visit that all my pooches are guard trained, and that while they pose no threat to normal actions, they might misinterpret behavior such as slapping me on the back. He told me, "No problem!" (a favorite expression of his), and we proceeded to ruminate about days of yore.

That evening, while we were discussing how best to rectify existing tax legislation, Fred slid off his chair onto the shag carpet, ostensibly to stretch out a bit. My eldest Doberman, Chattan, was a few feet away, gnawing a Nylabone. Forgetting or ignoring my warning, Fred, on all fours, began putting the sneak on the dog, stealthily advancing toward him. Sure, Fred was only "playing with the big black doggie." He intended no malice. To his mind he was engaged in an antic.

Now, I knew Chattan pretty well. It was easy to read that he wasn't going to react with a bite. A bark, doubtless, but not a bite. At least not right away. As Fred crept that final inch too close the Doberman exploded. Leaping over the bone and landed in his drive stance, his white teeth scant inches from Fred's nose, Chattan emitted a characteristically low,

Dobie rumble. It was a frozen moment. Seconds later, in a higher-than-normal voice, Fred beseechingly spoke my name.

Still seated in my recliner and struggling to maintain a straight face, I solemnly intoned, "Fred, I told you not to mess with my dogs. They view certain behavior as insulting and—as you can plainly see—inciting. You chose not to heed my counsel. Now, I'm going to go grab a soft drink from the fridge, and I've a suggestion that you'd do well to respect in my absence: Don't so much as blink."

No, I didn't leave Fred to the Doberman's tender mercies. I stood up and said, "C'mon, Chattan." The dog gave a disgusted snort, followed me from the room, and Fred collapsed with a thud onto the floor.

Before you decide I acted callously, consider a couple of points. First, had I reacted suddenly, such as jumping toward the dog to keep him back, my quick movement could have triggered him. It probably wouldn't have but it could have, and I wasn't willing to take the chance—things were just too explosive. Besides, Chattan was bereft of collar, and there's not much to grab on a Doberman—they're designed that way. Second, Fred learned something about dogs that may keep him safe in the future. Another canine might have reacted with teeth instead of threat. Last, and perhaps most important, the Doberman's behavior was proper. He was convinced the stranger was threatening him and he reacted in kind. I don't encourage threats myself, and there's no reason a dog should have to adopt a walk-all-over-me philosophy either, especially in his own home.

## Logistics

The owners didn't want their two female Salukis to heel in side-by-side fashion, but apart, Silk to the handler's right and Satin to the left. Other than my own occasional awkwardness, due to unfamiliarity with working a dog at my right, no problem arose until we came to the Finish.

In traditional brace work (handling two dogs simultaneously), both heel to the left. They Finish either Inside or Outside as the Recall doesn't mis-position them. Heeling a dog on each side, though, ill situates them for the Finish. Silk heeled to my right and Recalled toward my left. Satin heeled conventionally and Recalled toward my right. Teaching both the same manner of Finish was out of the question. The Inside move would have them bumping in to one another, and a dual Go-Around would have had them meeting behind me. Just enough tension existed between them that I was not wont to facilitate a confrontation (especially one that could occur *in proximo* to my backside).

I pondered various ways of solving the problem, including having them cross during the Recall. My solution was teaching Silk the Go-Around Finish, and Satin the Inside Flip. Since this required each animal to Finish away from the other, it kept them apart. It also created an impressive visual effect for their dazzled owners.

There's no great moral to this account. It's presented only as a study in technical problem-solving.

## Eclipse

This one's personal. Sure, they all are, but this one is greatly so. One issue that any dog owner must resolve is the passing of his or her best friend. The following is offered with the hope that it will help those in need weather that bleak time.

My German Shepherd Dog, Smokey, to whose memory this book is dedicated, was a member of my family for nearly five years. He died at the too-young age of nine, having been diagnosed as suffering from an incurable spinal disease a year earlier. Being given time to prepare was both a blessing and a curse. A blessing as we were able to spend a lot of time together, a curse in knowing that nothing could stave off the inevitable.

During those last months his coordination and balance melted away by inches. Day-to-day changes were almost imperceptible, yet it was obvious that he walked better in August than in September, and so on. Formerly a certified Police K-9, and always an active dog, the disease gradually robbed Smokey of the ability to do the things he loved most: Running, jumping, playing, long walks. Too, his spirit began to falter. His progressively more frequent stumbles embarrassed him. He felt shame for "less-than-my-best" acts that were, of course, the result of events beyond his ability to control or comprehend.

The hardest question was, "How long do I let this go on?" I struggled with the conflicting issues of quantity of life versus quality of living. Ultimately I resolved that so long as Smokey wasn't in pain, I'd not take one day from him. Watching his bit-by-bit deterioration was heartbreaking, but he was always happy and at peace just to be near me, and I felt I had no right to subtract so much as one minute rightfully his.

One Sunday the infirmity's progress—which was mercifully pain-free throughout—brought Smokey to the point where he could hardly walk. The vets had cautioned me that after he began to lose back-leg function, the disease's next stage would be one of unending agony. So at that point the question whether to put my friend to sleep was intellectually uncomplicated—no other option remained. Emotionally, however, choosing to let Smokey go was as painful a decision as I've ever endured. He trusted me right up to the end, finally trusting me to make the right choice.

I called the vet, he met Smokey and me at the office, we did the deed, and I came within a whisker of resolving to get out of dog-related activities altogether. Smokey and I had just been down too many roads together. We had taught each other much, had shared a special journey. Our bond was such that whenever I'd go from one room to another, he'd always be right there with me, even if he'd been in a sound sleep seconds before. It wasn't that he was a clinger—with me was where he felt he belonged, that's all.

For a long time afterward, home was an empty, hollow place. Acquaintances offered appreciated sympathies, friends gave me the space I needed to sort things out. It was only weeks before that Howell Book House had sent me a contract for the publication of *Dog Logic,* an event that had me sailing in the clouds. Smokey slipped away, and I learned about other clouds, the dark ones that permeate the abyss.

Doubtless many readers have had to endure a similar trial. It's part of the cost of canine friendship: the owner will usually outlive the dog. Too, the stronger the bond the deeper the pain. And though we know all that going in, that someday we'll have to go it alone, the anguish of lost contact and companionship gives a new meaning to the word, "nevermore."

Hoping that it helps you, an awareness that kept me going during that dark time—in addition to a belief that Smokey and I will meet again—was that my best friend had always radiated a never-give-up philosophy. His courage never flagged, even in situations that might have caused another to buckle. That's my way of saying he taught me much while he was alive, and after he wasn't. He showed me how to go on without him. Not happily, perhaps, but abidingly. I'm glad I was there to help ease him through as best I could, hugging him, whispering, "I love you," as he slipped away. Given the same situation I'd repeat the act tomorrow. Smokey was to the point that the agonies were closing in on him, the vets had done all they could, and no other choice was left me. What I did was sponsored by love, nothing more. It's part of the promise I make to any pet of mine—the animal will never want or suffer.

As stated in *Dog Logic,* "The drawback to having known such a fine animal is that an owner's perception . . . can be colored by [the dog's] memory. No other dog can . . . fill the void left in the lives of those he touched. If you've ever been blessed with such a pet, be thankful for the joy and warmth he brought you, but avoid cheapening the dog's memory'' by reacting to your loss with bitterness and anger. Your missing friend ''deserves a better epitaph.''

Messages: Appreciate what you've got while you've got it. When your Smokey leaves—as he someday must—let him go, with gratitude for the good times, for his company. No, I'm not saying you should try to forget. Denial's unhealthy. It catches up to a person. Besides, if you're anything like me, you couldn't shut out the memories even if you tried. I'm saying that you must avoid shackling yourself to yesterday. That's costly grieving as it robs you of today and tomorrow, of the joy of knowing other friends, other loves. Reduced to its simplest terms, death is loss, loss is change and any change is stressful by definition. It's a painful time and that's normal; it's to be expected and lived through. Rather than feign indifference, acknowledge the sadness, and know that any eclipse is temporary; that it eventually ends, naturally, if one lets it.

## Contact

I had responded to the nursing home's invitation to stage an obedience demonstration with Chattan, my Number One Doberman, and to discuss why *Canis familiaris* is known as ''man's best friend.'' During our presentation I noticed an elderly man in a wheelchair, staring unseeing into the distance. It was as though his body was present but his spirit was elsewhere.

After running Chattan through several routines, I led the Doberman among the thirty or so folks in attendance. This is generally the high point of such events for the audience (and for me): those attending being allowed to pet a ''killer Doberman,'' and receiving an occasional cheek slurp in response. During our walk through the group, I caught an attendant's eye and nodded toward the wheelchair-bound gentleman. The aide shook her head negatively, whispering as I passed, ''He doesn't communicate.''

So what does one do? Ignore the old man? Just pass him by? Act as though he doesn't exist? Figuring that he could tune out Chattan and me if he wished, but that I wasn't going to make the decision for him, I said ''Good morning'' as we drew close. Reacting to the lack of response, the Dobe glanced my way for direction. ''Go say 'Hi,' '' I told the dog, gesturing toward the individual. Chattan advanced and rooted his muzzle under the veined hand, as he often does with me to get some loving.

Presently the old man looked down at the dog. The dog peered upward at the old man. What next occurred is difficult to put into words— suffice it to say that something passed between them, something almost tangible. Contact happened. It was as though they'd known one another forever. As the elderly gentleman slowly began to caress the back of Chattan's neck, a mild shiver ran up my spine. The dog, merely by his presence, had done what humans had been unable to achieve. I decided to skip my talk on "man's best friend." It was no longer necessary. There was nothing I could add.

Chattan and I have returned to the nursing home several times since. The old gentleman is always glad to see the Dobe, and vice versa, but he's yet to say anything to me. I'm not sure he knows I'm there. But that's not important.

## A Question of Determining Guilt

I had to hold the telephone receiver away from my ear: the reverberations of a howling child and a yelling adult were deafening. The lady told me her eight-month-old Miniature Schnauzer had just bitten her five-year-old child, and, "I want you to give me one good reason why I shouldn't get rid of this dog right here and now!"

After determining that the pup was currently vaccinated for rabies, I inquired if this was a first-time occurrence. It was. Until now the dog and the little boy were best friends. "Why did the animal bite?" I asked. The caller replied she didn't see it happen, but that the child claimed, "Lady bit me for no reason." Knowing that dogs don't do anything without motivation, I suggested the woman allow the youngster to calm down, then ferret out additional details about the incident, and call me back.

An hour later the phone rang. "Well, it wasn't Lady's fault after all. Jeffrey had watched some fool cartoon character on TV toss a dog in the air, and he figured he'd try it himself. He frightened Lady, he understands that now. They're outside playing, and I think everything'll be okay. I may get rid of the TV, though."

In a nutshell, the Schnauzer had acted out of self-defense. Experience teaches that when a family pet with no history of biting does nail someone, especially a family member, often the person did something he shouldn't have done. Should you ever be faced with a similar situation, make very sure you have the straight story before taking any action.

## The "Pro"

The trainer was from Germany. His arrival had been heralded by seminar organizers as an event akin to the Second Coming. As I'd already entered the Schutzhund trial scheduled to precede the weekend clinic, I decided to attend. It's easy to grow stale in my business—trainers can unknowingly get set in their ways—and it sounded like a fun getaway.

After the seminar's first fifteen or twenty minutes, it was obvious the Deutschlander knew *Canis familiaris*. His reading of dogs was impressive, and even given the language barrier, he was an accomplished instructor and an amusing showman. Then things took a negative turn.

After taking the German Shepherd Dog's leash from the owner, the trainer commanded, "Fuss." Up to this point he'd been making brisk commands, but this time his sound was more of a soft grunt. The dog, sitting facing the trainer, didn't move. Save for a reactive flinch of uncertainty—a canine equivalent of "Say what?"—pooch made no attempt to Finish. It was obvious, to me at least, that the animal had no idea what he was supposed to do and was seeking clearer instruction.

In a flash the Shepherd Dog was airborne as the visiting expert leash-tossed him to the Heel position. The man then commanded, "Fuss," sharply this time, and began walking at a typically quick pace. The dog, who moments before had been a picture of confidence and pride, now slunk along in whipped-dog fashion. While this elicited a chorus of "Ahs!" from some of those gathered, I decided I'd seen enough abuse for one morning and went for coffee. Once on the road, I further decided that no restaurant can hold a candle to home-brewed, and I headed back to Wyoming.

I've attended seminars where I didn't agree with the instructor's every utterance. Dog training is a highly individualistic art, and, as stated in *Dog Logic*'s Preface, method and approach are largely a matter of "opinion and conjecture." But when confronted with such blatant, center-stage mishandling, which was nothing less than cruelty as it put a willing but confused, helpless animal in a no-win situation, I intervene when possible, or get gone in protest when it isn't.

## Setup

Prior to competing in a Schutzhund trial, an acquaintance told me that he'd come up with a gimmick for increasing his dog's fire in performing the Send-Away. The term "gimmick" bothered me somewhat, but I turned an attentive ear. Schutzhund Send-Aways can be a pitfall, given that a dog has to run on command in a straight line from the handler, and continue running until directed to lie down. The distance involved is often one hundred yards.

"Joel, you know that we can align the dog at heel repeatedly, till he's satisfactorily positioned, using as many commands as we want without losing points because the exercise doesn't officially begin until we tell the judge we're ready. Right?''

"That's my understanding of the rules, yes," I responded.

"Well, I've taught my Rotty that after I've commanded him to 'Heel' three times in a row, with me making a slight adjustment in position each time, getting him just so, the next thing I'm going to do is heel a few steps and send him away. It sets up the dog's mind for what's coming, and he takes off like a shot. The judge'll love it.''

A training guideline I follow is never to let a dog know what the next command will be, especially during competition. An intelligent canine learns patterns quickly enough as it is, and command-anticipation can sink an otherwise successful outing. My opinion hadn't been sought, however, so other than a ''Break a leg!'' bit of well-wishing, I kept my mouth shut.

The following day the gentleman and his Rottweiler heeled to the starting point for the Send-Away. Sure enough, he commanded the dog, ''Heel,'' three separate times, ostensibly positioning his companion each time. He then commanded, ''Heel,'' again, the team began moving, and after two or three steps the Rott took off like a shot, indeed. The only problem was that the handler had yet to give the Send-Away command. I was standing near enough to the judge to overhear his comment to the trial chairman: ''Beautiful Send-Out. Too bad the dog did it on his own. Zero score.''

Gimmicks are deceptive by nature, and while this or that oddball technique may be helpful in oddball situations, they have a way of backfiring when used in normal circumstances.

### Stormy Dog, Mild Owner

Chang's problem was twofold: borderline unstable temperament, and an owner who feared him. Starting when the Akita was seven months old, attempts at governing his behavior had elicited bared-teeth growling. Harvey, the dog's gentle owner, invariably responded by backing off. Lack of follow-through reinforced the dog's belligerence, of course, essentially telling him he could get away with it. When Chang arrived for training I had my hands full. Not just with the year-old Akita—with the owner, too.

As you'll see, straightening out Chang as to who was *Alpha* wasn't all that difficult. Moments after meeting and getting a reading on him, it was obvious that he was trainable and that his aggressiveness was mostly a product of learning. If the problem was genetically rooted, it was weakly so. The base difficulty lay with Harvey, who was ill-suited for this particular canine. His reaction to Chang's threats amounted to "Oh, my goodness," and a swift retreat. Had Harvey been emotionally constituted to send a message of "Dog, you are about to find yourself in deep trouble," the problem would have been resolved, but such was not Harvey's way.

Chang was my first concern. I went after his "Put-'em-up!" proclivity with my *sweet-and-sour technique*. Simply put, after very gently teaching, "Sit" and "Fuss," deflectively enduring the Akita's minor complaints during the process, I later purposefully triggered his aggression at a time and place of *my* choosing. That's the safest way to confront an on-the-fight dog.

As outlined in *Dog Logic*, should a large pooch impede the trainer during a heeling left-turn, the response is to knee the offender out of the way. Also mentioned is the caution that the technique can light an aggressive animal's fuse. I did, and it did. Up Chang came, all teeth and spit, ready to put me in my place. Of course, since I was reasonably sure how he'd respond, I had the animal's room ready for him, so to speak.

I seized neck-fur and skin (but not the windpipe) under the jaw, and raised Chang onto his back tippy-toes, eye-level with me. I ran him backward, driving my knees into his underside while cuffing his muzzle with my free hand and repeatedly telling him, "No!" I then pitched him onto all fours, commanded, "Fuss," and a mortified Akita and a relieved trainer heeled away. The battle was done in seconds, and we got along fine from that day on.

Harsh treatment? Sure, though the adjective is pejorative. Cruel? Not by a long shot. Cruel would have been halfway measures that would have taught Chang that I—like Harvey—could be had. Mollycoddling would have guaranteed having to really land on him later. Anyhow, the Akita learned rapidly, and the power of praise clarified his status in the pack, communicating that his obedience was valuable and appreciated. We became pals. Now to the problem of Harvey.

To transfer training successfully from one human to another, one condition must be fulfilled: the person who didn't train the dog must maintain the same level of firmness and praise as did the trainer. Otherwise the obedience vanishes, taking respect and rapport with it.

Though Harvey's heart was in the right place, Chang was too much dog for him. Failing a reversal in the man's personality and perspective, there was no way that gentle soul could ever handle this particular dog. If training were a cookie-cutter function, transforming a canine into a wind-him-up-and-watch-him-obey-anyone robot, there'd have been no problem. But, of course, training doesn't work like that (thank Heaven). If it did, there'd be no "dog" left; only a scrubbed-and-vacuumed, hollow, furry shell without a soul.

I called Harvey and arranged a meeting. He arrived, we observed the amenities, and I made the following, well-rehearsed if nervously delivered speech.

"Harvey, this animal is more than you can handle. He always will be. His training will transfer to someone as tough as he is, but you aren't that person. You're inherently as gentle as Chang is formidable. A dog should share your life, but Chang simply isn't that dog. It's hard saying these things to you, but it's part of what you're paying me for. Now, what must we do here?"

Harvey surprised me. He sighed (in relief, as it turned out), told me such had been his feeling all along, and that he'd become surer while Chang was away. He felt he and Chang were no longer right for each other; that they hadn't been for some time. "You think you're giving me bad news, but to me it's good news. I'd felt guilty just thinking about giving Chang up, but you just took me off the hook." Then it was my turn to sigh in relief.

You have to understand, dealing with ninety-plus pounds of hostile dog is a low-pressure situation for me. No, I don't like it, but I'd rather do that anytime than have to tell someone who's reared an animal from puppyhood that the two of them should part company. That's real pressure, the kind that's difficult to deal with. Yet, in training someone's dog you have an obligation to be true to both dog and owner. I could have collected my fee, relinquished the leash, wished them well and said, "Ta, ta." But that's not only a wrong way to operate, ethically and morally, such an attitude will eventually sink a business.

Epilogue: With Harvey's permission I contacted someone I felt would be right for Chang. She made arrangements with Harvey, and today the Akita and his new *Alpha* are best friends. I helped Harvey locate a more complimentary canine companion, and they've become inseparable. Cinderella endings are rare, but they are truly gratifying.


## Stay-Steady?

The student, a likeable but cocky sort, assured us his Afghan Hound was rock-solid on Stays. He challenged my visiting friend, a trainer. "Five bucks says any reasonable distraction won't make him break. You get one try and one try only. Go ahead."

"Okay," my visitor replied, "command him to Stay." He did.

"Now, without a normal-speed, walk-away start, leave your dog by taking off at a dead run."

My trainer/friend donated her winnings to the local animal shelter. No, she's not clairvoyant. She just knows how easy it is to overlook the obvious when laying out a conditioning program. Trainers routinely *walk* from their dogs after commanding, "Stay." It seldom occurs to them to run. When a person *needs* his pet to remain in place, the change in pattern—running away—can draw the dog along. The student had done a good job of conditioning his companion for all manner of environmental distractions—gunfire, crowds, traffic, the lot—but he'd not enhanced the "Stay" concept. It must be absolute, despite not only nearby happenings but whatever the trainer does after giving the command.

### "One Inch Tougher Than the Dog"

The Greyhound wouldn't retrieve over a high jump. She'd leap over the obstacle to pursue the dumbbell, but invariably she'd return around one end of the hurdle. The owner had tried several tactics to eradicate the problem, from blocking each end with lawn furniture—which the hound also went around—to light-lining the dog over the jump, which often caught on a support, toppling the structure. The dog perceived her owner's intent, and she was playing with the lady's head. Latent *Alpha* struggles had resurfaced, and CDX competition was less than a week away.

Fortunately, the owner could easily lift her dog. She lowered the jump to one-half normal height (to facilitate the upcoming task and reduce the risk of injury), then threw the dumbbell and commanded, "Bring." The Greyhound sailed over the jump, snatched up the dumbbell, and started to return around one end. "No!" her owner boomed. The dog stopped in her tracks. Advancing quickly the lady snatched up her dog. "I said, 'Bring!' " she admonished, and she tossed her pet, dumbbell and all, over the jump. "Good Bring," she said as she ran around the jump to the chagrined hound. Then the owner again hurled the dumbbell over the jump. On the command, "Bring," the dog performed beautifully. With praise ringing in her ears, we ended the session. They earned the CDX in three straight shows.

Not only was the "one-inch-tougher-than-the-dog" concept in use, but the lesson was applied in a personal sense. It had to be. There wasn't time for a fade-out, habit-formation process. The Greyhound had to believe she'd be tossed over a CDX-ring jump anytime she goofed. Based on the outcome, I'd say the dog expected her owner would have done just that.

196

## Helper

Pursuing a tennis ball is among my dogs' favorite activities. It not only outlets their "Get-the-rabbit!" need, it's good exercise. While sometimes I play with a pooch singly, the group also enjoys pack action, such as when I simultaneously hurl a ball for each. The game's object is to grab the toy and return to me ahead of other competitors. The practice indirectly reinforces a positive mind-set toward Recalls and Retrieving, but more important, it heightens attraction and bonding.

My new five-month-old puppy, Chaska, kept losing sight of her target. She'd momentarily break concentration on her toy to watch another chaser, and when she'd look back, she couldn't see her own ball. By then it had come to rest, and dogs don't see stationary objects as well as moving ones. Once she'd lost track of the toy she'd come to me, looking for help. Frustration was beginning to demoralize her. The others won a prize, she didn't.

One solution would have been to leave Chaska out of the game until her concentration matured. That smacked of sweeping dust under the rug, though, and while I was cerebrating my way through the dilemma, another of my Dobermans, Chattan, resolved it.

He'd seen me guide Chaska to her toy, to help her avoid failure, albeit she was achieving a "lesser-than" victory. Exactly what Chattan concluded I cannot say, but I can report that whenever Chaska couldn't find her ball, he'd trot to it and stand in place until she got the idea. Over time he modified his action to running to her toy, circling it once, and departing, making Chaska have to react more quickly to his message. Later, he'd only stare at her toy from a distance, and finally he quit sending any cue. By then his young friend had learned.

An idea offered in the distraction-proofing section of Chapter 1 is, "If you're training more than one dog, use him, or her, or them." An extension of that philosophy is, "If you're training more than one dog, *let* him, or her, or them help." Don't get in the middle of a good situation. Nature programs dogs to respond first and foremost to other dogs. When it's to your advantage, let it happen. And count your blessings.

## Closure

As you and your dog continue to grow and learn, pay heed to his or her messages. Ponder the seemingly little things. Don't settle for sluff-off, "Wonder what that means?" reactions on your part. Pursue the

"Why?"'s relentlessly. In addition to being your best friend, a gifted teacher is at the end of your leash.

This chapter continues in *Kennels and Kenneling*.

## Reflection

A dog will readily, and happily, comply with any reasonable request. He usually knows already how to do it. The trainer, however, must formulate the request in a manner that is understood by the dog.

Dietmar Schellenberg,
*Top Working Dogs—A Training Manual*

# Postscript

$\mathbf{A}$DVANCEMENT to higher training levels offers many rewards for dog and trainer alike. Not only can both share in more activities, rapport expands exponentially as each ventures further into the other's universe, together creating an indefatigable oneness. Reliability becomes a given, doors previously closed spring open, freedom exists in its purest form.

There are several keys to advanced obedience, but the major one appears in the book's *Preface*: ". . . by the time a person reaches this level, he either has something going with his dog, or he probably never will without considerable restructuring." The lifeblood of rapport-based training is bonding, which—with respect to dog training—is perhaps the oldest form of communication between man and dog. True, domination is essential to the human-canine relationship. Though it can seem paradoxical from human perspective, to dominate a dog is to provide the animal with ultimate security. At the same time, the phrase "to dominate" is not interchangeable with "to violate," "to enslave" or "to rule through fear."

More years ago than I care to remember, a trainer remarked to me, "The farther you go, the easier it gets." At the time her words seemed a contradiction. Then a very special dog came my way, and he filled in the blanks for me. He taught me that the "it" the trainer referred to wasn't training, but bonding, and that as bonding grows, training at any level becomes easier.

I hope what you read here has provided the specific knowledge you sought, whether we're talking distraction proofing, off-leash training, competition or dealing with dog problems. But of greater importance, if this book has helped bring you and pooch closer, then it has served its purpose, for both of us.

The dog's love is unconditional, his trust absolute. Remember who he is, always, for both your sakes.

# Glossary

THE FOLLOWING TERMS are defined within the context of dog training and related concepts. In some instances, the definitions bear little resemblance to those found in a general dictionary of the English language. The descriptions have been kept as simple and nontechnical as possible.

**Active resistance**   Overt resistance by a dog to a trainer's intent.

**AKC (American Kennel Club)**   A governing body whose primary area of responsibility is the maintenance of purebred canine bloodlines in the United States.

**Alpha**   Pack leader; number-one animal; the boss.

**Animation**   Overt canine enjoyment.

**Anthropomorphism**   Assigning human values and traits to another species. This commonly occurs when one compares the training of dogs to the rearing of children.

**Anticipation**   Canine performance of a command before the command is given.

**Attitude**   Canine behavior revealing the animal's feeling about a command's directive, or of a situation or event.

**Attraction**   Level of canine interest and trust in his handler(s).

**Automatic Sit**   An obedience basic requiring a dog to sit because an event occurs: i.e., during Heeling, the handler stops walking; during a Recall or a Retrieve, the animal arrives at a position in front of and facing the handler.

**Avoidance conditioning** Aversive conditioning that allows a subject to avoid totally an unpleasant consequence by reacting properly to an environmental cue. This is a form of *Instrumental conditioning*.

**Backsliding** A short-lived phenomenon that sometimes occurs (usually during the third to fourth week of basic obedience training), whereby the animal appears to have forgotten nearly all lessons to date.

**Behavior—instinctual** Behavior motivated by knowledge with which a dog is born.

**Behavior—learned** Behavior motivated by knowledge a canine acquires through experience.

**Bluff** A training concept whereby a dog is led to believe that the handler has physical control over the animal even when he or she does not.

**Bonding** A process that causes a dog to sense deep attraction toward another animal, canine or human.

**Burned-out** Refers to the attitude of a dog whose training has been so prolonged and repetitious that he's lost interest in the work, and may have even developed an aversion toward it and/or the trainer.

**Carryover effect** The positive or negative influence upon canine perception of one activity by another.

**Challenge the dog** A training concept that attempts to bring out a dog's best efforts by making his tasks just difficult enough that he has to work at performing them.

**Choke collar** A training collar, usually fashioned of steel links, that can restrict and even terminate breathing if misused.

**CKC (Canadian Kennel Club)** A governing body whose primary area of responsibility is the maintenance of purebred canine bloodlines in Canada.

**Classical conditioning** Linking a natural biological response with an unnatural stimulus.

**Collar tab** A short length of cord or similar material that a trainer attaches to a collar's live ring, thereby providing a quick handle.

**Command** A trainer's directive to his dog that calls for a behavioral response from the animal.

**Communication** Exchange of information between two or more individuals, be they human or canine.

**Competition** Performance of learned behaviors against an ideal standard.

**Compulsion** Correction; external force; pressure.

**Concentration** Canine or human focused attention.

**Conditioning**
   1. Practicing lessons in varying situations.
   2. Methods of teaching: See also *Avoidance conditioning, Classical conditioning, Escape conditioning, Instrumental conditioning,* and *Operant conditioning.*

**Confrontation** Active and overt canine rebellion, usually symbolizing at least a partial struggle for dominance.

**Consistency**   Relating to a canine in an unchanging manner.

**Contact**   Any form of communication.

**Contention**   A canine act that indicates pronounced resistance to the trainer's intent.

**Correction**   Physical and/or verbal pressure applied by a trainer in response to his dog's disobedience.

**Correction match**   A competition event that simulates a dog show, and which allows handlers to correct their dogs in a ring setting.

**Critical periods**   Psychological developmental periods during puppyhood. See *The New Knowledge of Dog Behavior,* by Clarence Pfaffenberger (New York: Howell Book House; 1963).

**Crossover conditioning**   Similar to the *Spillover effect,* this training encourages a dog to transfer a positive attitude he has about a given article or thing to another article or thing.

**Cue**   See *Command.*

**Dead ring**   The ring of a training collar to which a trainer does not attach a leash. See also *Live ring.*

**Deflection**   Momentarily overlooking low-risk contention or a peripheral aspect of undesirable behavior in order to prevent either from escalating.

**Desensitization**   Systematically lessening anxiety-producing responses through gradual exposure to increasingly stressful stimuli.

**Distractions**   Stimuli that may entice a dog to break from command.

**Distraction proofing**   Exposing a dog to distractions, the purpose being to teach in a controlled setting that the animal must obey the trainer's commands despite nearby happenings.

**Dominance**   The stance from which a trainer must operate in order to assume the *Alpha* role.

**Dominant**   This refers to an animal who would rather lead than follow.

**Drive**
  1.   Behaviors that seek to satisfy instinctual demands.
  2.   A training technique that capitalizes upon a dog's instincts toward stimuli to which he is attracted.
  3.   A dog's degree of attraction toward a stimulus.

**Escape conditioning**   An aversive teaching method that allows a subject to avoid further unpleasant consequences without an environmental cue. This is quite similar to *Avoidance conditioning.*

**Extra-mile principle**   Requiring slightly more of a dog than the handler actually expects. Usually used in competition conditioning.

**Fear biter**   A dog who arrives at the *fight-or-flight* state with no more provocation than occurs during normal contact situations.

**Fear training**   A despicable training method that relies solely on teaching a dog to do certain things to avoid pressure, resulting in a whipped dog who acts like one, and whose training comes apart when confronted by that which he fears more than the so-called trainer.

**Fight or Flight**  The point in the stress cycle where a dog attempts to either attack or flee, rather than passively endure the situation causing the stress.

**Finish**  An obedience function through which a dog moves on command from a position in front of and facing his handler to the Heel position.

**Fire**  Canine exuberance.

**Focus**  The directing of mental concentration.

**Foundational**  Refers to an obedience lesson that is valuable not only for its own merits, but which is also a necessary element of a subsequent lesson.

**Fun match**  A competition event that simulates a dog show.

**Gender conflict**  This concept refers to a dog who doesn't relate well with others—be they human or canine—of the same sex.

**Handler**  See *Trainer*.

**Heel position**  A dog positioned squarely at his handler's left side with his shoulder adjacent to the handler's left leg.

**Heeling**  A canine's synchronous movement with his handler while maintaining the *Heel position*.

**I and the Not-I**  A dog's view of himself in relation to other beings.

**Identifiers**  Terms that a trainer assigns to objects and beings to create a language beyond commands with his pet.

**Independent**  A dog who would prefer to be by himself and on his own.

**Instinct**  General inborn urges to act in response to basic needs (survival, packlike social structuring, etc.).

**Instrumental conditioning**  A educational method in which a canine develops habits by learning from the consequences of his actions.

**Integration**  The phase of training during which exercises that heretofore have been practiced separately are performed in sequence, thus creating a dog's obedience repertoire.

**Intelligence**  The ability to thrive and problem-solve in any environment.

**Learned-helplessness syndrome**  Canine acceptance of abuse as a natural, unavoidable consequence of contact with humans.

**Learning**  A permanent behavioral change resulting from experience.

**Learning rate**  The speed with which an animal can absorb new material.

**Light lead**  A leash that is appreciably lighter than the primary leash.

**Light line**  A long, lightweight line used in off-leash training.

**Live ring**  The ring of a training collar to which a trainer attaches his or her leash. See also *Dead ring*.

**Misdirected anger**  Canine ire directed toward some object that is not the actual cause of the animal's resentment.

**Moment of recognition**  The instant at which a dog's aspect communicates, "Aha! I understand what my trainer is saying to me."

**Name**  A dog's appellation, which is more of a positively based attention-getter than a definition of self.

**Novice**

    **1.**   Either a trainer or a dog who is new to training.

    **2.**   The first of three obedience competition levels sanctioned by the American and Canadian Kennel Clubs.

**On-demand feeding**   Making food available for pooch at all times.

**Open**   The second of three levels of obedience competition sanctioned by the American and Canadian Kennel Clubs.

**Operant conditioning**   Teaching an active behavior in response to positive or negative stimuli.

**Ostrich defense**   One response of a frightened dog, turning his attention away from that which he fears—"If I can't see it, it can't hurt me."

**Pack**   The social structure of a dog's "family."

**Pack leader**   See *Alpha.*

**Passive resistance**   Covert canine resistance to a trainer's intent.

**Personality**   A canine's habitual manner of relating with his environment, and with individuals he contacts.

**Pinch collar**   A multilinked training device that imparts to a canine the sensation of teeth grabbing his neck.

**Play toy**   A special toy to which a dog is greatly attracted.

**Play work**   A concentration-building exercise (i.e., the Guard Game) rooted in positive-reinforcement techniques.

**Praise**   Affirmation; approval; communicating to a dog that his behavior is acceptable.

**Pressure**   See *Correction.*

**Put Down**   Canine euthanasia.

**Rapport**   An intangible that says to your pet, "I seek that which I project: respect and oneness."

**Recall**   A trainer's summoning of his dog to a position in front of and facing him.

**Reinforcement**   A stimulus that can cause a behavior change.

**Release cue**   A command that tells a canine that he is on his own for a time; that he is no longer under his handler's direction.

**Replacement**   A technique commonly used to halt destructive behavior whereby a dog is given an article to use for venting natural urges.

**Resistance**   See *Active resistance* and *Passive resistance.*

**Ring nerves**   A condition akin to stage fright, associated with competition.

**Ring-wise**   A blame-the-dog defense that seeks to transfer responsibility for determining if an animal is ready for competition from handler to dog. It supposedly describes a dog who's been shown so many times at a specific competition level that he's learned the handler cannot, or will not, correct in a ring setting.

**Schutzhund**   A form of competition wherein a dog must be proficient at tracking, obedience, and protection.

**Show lead** A lightweight leash commonly used in conformation showing.

**Sneak-biter** A dog who bites for enjoyment, but only after first projecting the lie that he indeed cares greatly for the person he intends to bite.

**Socialization** Introducing a dog (usually during puppyhood) to various environments, individuals and experiences.

**Spillover effect** The effect of a seemingly nonstructured lesson seeping into all areas of a dog's reliability.

**Stimulus** Perceived environmental information.

**Stress** Sustained factors that create psychological and/or physiological pressure within or on a dog.

**Submission** Acceptance of dominant behavior.

**Submissive** This refers to an animal who would rather follow than lead.

**Sweet-and-sour technique** Temporarily enduring minor canine hostility until the trainer is ready to address the behavior.

**Teachable moment** One of many times in a dog's life when he is more receptive to new learning than he is during other times.

**Temperament** Canine psychological soundness and stability.

**Temperament testing** Systematic evaluation of genetically based canine traits.

**Throw chain** A short, lightweight chain used as a compulsion device.

**Trainable** Refers to a dog who is responsive to instruction.

**Trainer** One who trains a canine.

**Training** A process through which one takes control of and enhances mutual bonding with a dog by developing a basis for and means of significant communication.

**Utility** The highest of three levels of obedience competition sanctioned by the American and Canadian Kennel Clubs.

**Verbal bridge** Used to time the moment of a trainer's pleasure or displeasure with a dog's actions.

**Willingness** The degree of inherent and/or learned enjoyment a dog has toward training.

**Withers** A canine's shoulders.

**Work concept** Teaching a dog that his obedience is a direct contribution to his pack's welfare.

**Working** A general term that relates to teaching, practicing, or applying learned exercises.

# References

T HE FOLLOWING is provided for your convenience and education. All titles are currently in print, though some editions are difficult to locate owing to their degree of specialization.

*A*

*Abnormalities of Companion Animals* (Foley)
*About Dogs* (Rossi)
*Active Years for Your Aging Dog* (Hirshhorn)
*Advanced Training Workbook: Open and Utility* (Carson and Coryell)
*Agility Dog, The* (Lewis)
*Agility Dog Training for All Breeds* (Kramer)
*All About Dog Shows* (Kohl)
*All About Guard Dogs* (Hirshhorn)
*All About Training the Family Dog* (Cree)
*Analysis of Lost Person Behavior* (Syrotuck)
*Atlas of Dog Breeds of the World* (Wilcox and Walkowicz)
*Art of Raising a Puppy, The* (Monks of New Skete)

# B

*Basic Dog Training* (Watson)
*Basic Guide to Canine Nutrition* (Gaines)
*Basic Training and Care of Military Dogs* (Dept. of the Army)
*Basic Training Workbook: Novice* (Carson and Coryell)
*Behavior Problems in Dogs* (Campbell)
*Best Foot Forward* (Handler)
*Best Way to Train Your Gun Dog, The* (Tarrant)
*Beyond Basic Obedience Training* (Bauman)
*Blanche Saunders Obedience Training Courses* (Saunders)
*Body Language and Emotions of Dogs, The* (Milani)
*Book of Dogs, The* (Canadian Kennel Club)

# C

*Canine Anatomy* (Adams)
*Canine Clan, The* (McLaughlin)
*Canine Clinic* (Clarke)
*Canine Hip Dysplasia* (Lanting)
*Canine Reproduction* (Holst)
*Canines and Coyotes* (Almerall)
*Caring for Your Older Dog* (Berman and Landesman)
*Celebration of Dogs, A* (Caras)
*Chosen Puppy, The* (Benjamin)
*Collins Guide to Dog Nutrition, The* (Collins)
*Companion Dog Training* (Tossutti)
*Complete Book of Dog Health, The* (Animal Medical Center)
*Complete Book of Dog Obedience, The* (Saunders)
*Complete Book of Dogs, The* (Ensminger)
*Complete Book of Dog Training and Care* (McCoy)
*Complete Dog Book, The* (American Kennel Club)
*Complete Guard and Attack Dog Manual, The* (Smith)
*Complete Herbal Book for the Dog, The* (Levy)
*Complete Puppy and Dog Book* (Johnson and Galin)
*Controlling Your Dog Away from You* (Romba)
*Country Life Book of Dogs, The* (Lampson)

# D

*Delinquent Dogs: The Reform School Handbook* (Wilkinson)
*Deutsche Schutzhundschule* (Grewe)
*Dog, The: Historical, Psychological, Personality Study* (Perlson)
*Dog Anatomy Illustrated* (Way)
*Dog Behavior: The Genetic Basis* (Scott and Fuller)
*Dog Breeding for Professionals* (Richards)
*Dog Days* (Bernard)
*Dog Days: Other Times, Other Dogs* (White)
*Dog for the Kids, A* (Siegal)
*Dog in Action, The* (Lyons)
*Dog in the Family* (Dangerfield)
*Dog Locomotion and Gait Analysis* (Brown)
*Dog Logic* (McMains)
*Doglopaedia, The* (White)
*Dog-Master System, The* (Miller)
*Dog Obedience Training Manual* (Braund)
*Dog of Your Own, A* (Stoneridge)
*Dog Owner's Home Veterinary Handbook* (Carlson and Giffin)
*Dog Owner's Guide* (Kasco)
*Dog Problems* (Benjamin)
*Dog Psychology: The Basis of Dog Training* (Whitney)
*Dog Repair Handbook, The* (Nelson)
*Dog Showing* (Vanacore)
*Dogs* (Pearcy)
*Dogs* (Wratten)
*Dogs Are People, Too* (Miller)
*Dogs—Breeding and Showing* (Sutton)
*Dogs for Police Service* (Watson)
*Dogs: How to Train and Show Them* (Harmar)
*Dogs in Philosophy* (Donovan)
*Dogs in Shakespeare* (Donovan)
*Dog's Life, A: A Year in the Life of a Dog Family* (Burton/Allaby)
*Dogs of the American Frontier* (Pferd)
*Dogs of the American Indians* (Pferd)
*Dogs of the World: An Illustrated Encyclopedia* (Bongianni & Mori)
*Dogs Self Trained—Basic* (Self)
*Dogs Self Trained—Advanced* (Self)
*Dogsteps* (Elliott)
*Dog Tales: How to Solve Behavior Problems* (McSoley)
*Dogs That Work for a Living* (Brown)
*Dog Stories* (Herriot)

*Dogs Through History* (Riddle)
*Dog Training for Boys and Girls* (Saunders)
*Dog Training for Kids* (Benjamin)
*Dog Training for Law Enforcement* (Eden)
*Dog Training Guide* (Kenworthy)
*Dog Training Made Easy* (Tucker)
*Dog Tricks* (Haggerty and Benjamin)
*Dog Trivia* (Doherty)
*Dogwatching* (Morris)
*Domestic Animal Behavior* (Houpt and Wolski)
*Don't Shoot the Dog* (Pryor)
*Dynamics of Canine Gait* (Hollenbeck)


# E

*Electronic Dog Training* (Tortora)
*Encyclopedia of Veterinary Medicine, The* (Hart)
*Especially Dogs* (Taber)
*Euthanasia of the Companion Animal* (Press)
*Evans Guide for Civilized City Canines, The* (Evans)
*Evans Guide for Housetraining Your Dog, The* (Evans)
*Evans Guide to Counseling Dog Owners, The* (Evans)
*Everyday Dog* (Johnson)
*Expert Obedience Training for Dogs* (Strickland)
*Eyes That Lead, The* (Tucker)


# F

*Farmer's Dog, The* (Holmes)
*Find It! A Complete Guide to Scent Retrieving* (English)
*First Aid and Nursing Your Dog* (Edgson and Gwynne-Jones)
*First Aid for Dogs* (Whitney)
*Friend to Friend/Dogs That Help Mankind* (Schwartz)


# G

*Games Pets Play* (Fogle)
*Genetics and Social Behavior of the Dog* (Scott and Fuller)
*Genetics for Dog Breeders* (Robinson)
*Genetics of the Dog* (Willis)
*Go Find!* (Davis)

*Good Dog! The Basic Training Book for All Breeds* (Howell)
*Grid Search Techniques* (Syrotuck)
*Guard Dog, The* (Mundis)
*Guide to All-Breed Dog Showing, The* (Kohl and Goldstein)
*Guide to Junior Showmanship, A* (Simmons)
*Gun Dog* (Wolters)
*Gundog Training* (Erlandson)
*Gundogs: Their History, Breeding, and Training* (Petrie-Hay)
*Gundogs: Training and Field Trials* (Moxon)

## H

*Handbook of Veterinary Procedures* (Birk and Bistner)
*Happy Dog, Happy Owner* (Siegal)
*Home Grooming Guide for Dogs, The* (Yorinks)
*Howell Book on Puppy Raising* (Schwartz)
*How Puppies Are Born* (Prine)
*How to Be Your Dog's Best Friend* (The Monks of New Skete)
*How to Breed Dogs* (Whitney)
*How to Feed Your Dog* (Turner)
*How to Raise a Dog* (Kinney and Honeycutt)
*How to Raise a Puppy You Can Live With* (Rutherford)
*How to Speak Dog* (Flynn)
*How to Talk to Your Dog* (George)
*How to Train a Guard Dog* (Larson)
*How to Train a Watchdog* (Sessions)
*How to Train Dogs for Police Service* (Rapp)
*How to Train Hunting Dogs* (Brown)
*How to Train Your Dog* (Palmer)
*How to Train Your Dog in Six Weeks* (Landesman and Berman)
*How to Trim, Groom, and Show Your Own Dog* (Saunders)
*Hows and Whys of Psychological Dog Training* (Meisterfeld)
*Hunting Dogs: Questions and Answers* (Scott)

## I

*Illustrated Guide to Dog Diseases* (The TV Vet)
*Improving the Obedience Dog* (Self)
*Improve Your Handling* (Morsell)
*Inheritance of Coat Color in Dogs, The* (Little)
*Interrelations Between People and Pets* (Fogle)
*It's Magic* (Bishop)

# J

*Junior Showmanship* (Boyer)

# K

*Kennelwood Basic Training Manual* (Kennelwood, Inc.)
*Kennelwood Conformation Training Manual* (Kennelwood, Inc.)
*Kennelwood Puppy Manual* (Kennelwood, Inc.)
*Koehler Method of Dog Training, The* (Koehler)
*Koehler Method of Guard Dog Training, The* (Koehler)
*Koehler Method of Open Obedience, The* (Koehler)
*Koehler Method of Training Tracking Dogs, The* (Koehler)
*Koehler Method of Utility Dog Training, The* (Koehler)

# L

*Land Search Probabilities* (Syrotuck)
*Lassie Method, The* (Weatherwax)
*Leader Dogs for the Blind* (Gibbs)
*Lew Burke's Dog Training* (Burke)
*Love in the Lead* (Putnam)

# M

*Making Friends—Training Your Dog Positively* (Colflesh)
*Man & Dog/Psychology of Relationship* (Bergler)
*Manhunters! Hounds of the Big T* (Tolhurst and Reed)
*Man Meets Dog* (Lorenz)
*Mating and Whelping of Dogs* (Portman and Graham)
*Max—The Dog That Refused to Die* (Wayne)
*Medical and Genetic Aspects of Purebred Dogs* (Clark and Stainer)
*Military Working Dog Program Training Manual* (U.S. Air Force)
*Modern Dog Encyclopedia, The* (Davis)
*Mongrel* (Patmore)
*More Than a Friend: Dogs with a Purpose* (Siegal and Koplan)
*Mr. Lucky's Trick Dog Training Book* (Mr. Lucky)
*Mush!* (Sierra Nevada Dog Drivers, Inc.)

# N

*NASA Protection Manual* (North American Schutzhund Association)
*NASA Tracking Manual* (North American Schutzhund Association)
*Natural Method of Dog Training, The* (Whitney)
*Natural Way to Train Your Dog, The* (Benjamin)
*New Art of Breeding Better Dogs, The* (Onstott)
*New Dog Encyclopedia* (Davis)
*New Dogsteps, The* (Elliott)
*New Complete Junior Showmanship Handbook* (Brown and Mason)
*New Knowledge of Dog Behavior, The* (Pfaffenberger)
*New Standard Book on Dog Care and Training* (Cross and Saunders)
*Nicholas Guide to Dog Judging, The* (Nicholas)
*No Bad Dogs* (Woodhouse)
*No Force Method of Dog Training, The: Book 1* (Brown)
*No Force Method of Dog Training, The: Book 2* (Brown)
*Nop's Trial* (McCaig)

# O

*Obedience and Security Training for Dogs* (Scott)
*Obedience Class Instruction for Dogs* (Strickland)
*Obedient Dog, The* (Holmes)
*Of Wolves and Men* (Lopez)
*Olfaction and Odours* (McCartney)
*Our Friendly Animals and Whence They Came* (Schmidt)
*Owner's Guide to Better Behavior in Cats and Dogs* (Campbell)

# P

*Pearsall Guide to Successful Dog Training, The* (Pearsall)
*Perfect Puppy, The—How to Choose a Dog Through Behavior* (Hart)
*Personality of the Dog, The* (Aymar and Sagarin)
*Pet Care—The Complete Book* (Roach)
*Pet Loss and Human Bereavement* (Iowa State University Press)
*Pet Owner's Guide to Dogs* (White)
*Planned Breeding* (Brackett)
*Play-Training Your Dog* (Burnham)
*Police Dogs: Training and Care* (Her Majesty's Stationery Office)
*Police Service Dog, The* (Grewe)

*Popular Guide to Puppy-Rearing* (Gwynne-Jones)
*Positively Obedient* (Handler)
*Practical Dog Breeding and Genetics* (Frankling)
*Practical Education of the Bird Dog* (Antunano)
*Practical Hunter's Dog Book, The* (Falk)
*Practical Training for Big Dogs* (Dodd & Bygrave)
*Professional Dog Training* (Davis)
*Psyche of the Dog* (Radakovic)
*Puppies* (Spink)
*Puppy Manners* (Self)
*Puppy Training and Care, Revised* (Riddle)

# R

*Retriever Gun Dogs* (Brown)
*Retriever Training* (Scales)
*Retriever Working Certificate Training* (Rutherford and Branstad)
*Rappid Obedience and Watchdog Training* (Rapp)

# S

*Scenting and Nosework for Dogs* (Cree)
*Scent and the Scenting Dog* (Syrotuck)
*Scent: Training to Track, Search and Rescue* (Verbruggen)
*Schutzhund: Theory and Training Methods* (Barwig and Hilliard)
*Schutzhund Helper's Manual* (Leamer)
*Schutzhund Protection Training* (Petterson)
*Search and Rescue Dog Training* (Bryson)
*Second-Hand Dog* (Benjamin)
*Secrets of Show Dog Handling* (Miglioroni)
*Sheepdog: Its Work and Training, The* (Longton and Hart)
*Sheepdog Training* (Taggart)
*Show Dog, The* (Brucker)
*Slave to a Pack of Wolves* (Smith)
*Solving Your Dog Problems* (Tucker)
*Standard Book of Dog Breeding, The* (Grossman)
*Successful Dog Breeding* (Wilcox)
*Successful Dog Showing* (Forsyth)
*Superdog: Raising the Perfect Canine Companion* (Fox)

# T

*Teaching Dog Obedience Classes* (Volhard and Fisher)
*The Dog: Structure and Movement* (Smythe)
*Tickner's Dogs* (Tickner)
*Top Working Dogs, Revised* (Schellenberg)
*Toward the PhD for Dogs* (Martin and Chagnon)
*Tracking Dog* (Johnson)
*Tracking Trainer's Handbook* (Johnson)
*Training Dogs* (Most)
*Training Dogs with Common Sense* (Goodman and Czarnecki)
*Training Guard and Protection Dogs* (Dobson)
*Training Pointing Dogs* (Long)
*Training the Alsatian—German Shepherd* (Cree)
*Training the Competitive Working Dog* (Rose and Patterson)
*Training the Dog for Guard Work* (Arundel)
*Training the Family Dog* (Kaehele)
*Training the Retriever, A Manual* (Kersley)
*Training the Roughshooter's Dog* (Moxon)
*Training Spaniels* (Irving)
*Training Your Dog* (Volhard and Fisher)
*Training Your Dog for Birdwork* (Rafe)
*Training Your Dog to Win Obedience Titles* (Morsell)
*Training Your Retriever* (Free)
*Travels with Charley* (Steinbeck)
*Twenty-One Days to a Trained Dog* (Maller and Feinman)
*2000 Tips on Dog Care* (Reel)

# U

*Understanding Your Dog* (Fox)

# W

*Water Dog* (Wolters)
*Well Dog Book, The* (McGinnis)
*What's Bugging Your Dog: Canine Parasitology* (Schneider)
*When Good Dogs Do Bad Things* (Siegal and Margolis)
*What All Good Dogs Should Know* (Volhard and Bennett)
*Wild Dogs in Life and Legend* (Riddle)
*Working Dogs* (Humphrey and Warner)

*Working Sheepdogs, Management and Training* (Templeton & Mundell)
*Working Terriers* (Hobson)
*World of Sled Dogs* (I.S.D.R.A. and Coppinger)
*Why Does Your Dog Do That?* (Bergman)


*Y*


*Yes Dog, That's Right!* (Eckstein and Eckstein)
*Your Dog and the Law* (Loring)
*Your Dog and You* (Trumler)
*Your Dog, Companion and Helper* (Pearsall)
*Your Dog from Puppyhood to Old Age* (Rine)
*Your Dog—His Health and Happiness* (Vine)
*Your Dog, Its Development, Behavior and Training* (Rogerson)


*Periodicals*


Dog World (29 North Wacker Drive; Chicago IL 60606)
Dog Sports (P.O. Box 1167; Tracy, CA 95376)
DVG America (P.O. Box 314; Republic, MO 65738)
Front and Finish (P.O. Box 333; Galesburg, IL 61401)
NASA News (7318 Brennans Drive; Dallas, TX 75214)
Off-Lead (P.O. Box 307; Westmoreland, NY 13490)
Pure-Bred Dogs—American Gazette (51 Madison Avenue; New York, NY
    10010)
Schutzhund USA (1926 Hillman Avenue; Belmont, CA 94002)


Many individual breed texts are also available. For example, at least ten
books are in print about the German Shepherd Dog and over a dozen
about the Doberman Pinscher. With a little research you can learn what
is available on your breed(s) of choice.


216

# Index

Aborted Retrieve
  rationale, 115
  teaching, 116
Abused canines, 44
Active resistance, 201
Aggression toward humans
  biting a family member, 191
  inadvertent reinforcement, 177
*Alpha*, 161, 162, 178, 180, 193, 195, 196, 201
American Kennel Club (AKC), 201
Animation, 201
Anthropomorphism, 201
Anticipation, 201
Attitude, 201
Attraction, 201
Automatic Sit, 201
Avoidance conditioning, 202

Backsliding, 202
Behavior
  instinctual, 202
  learned, 202
Bluff concept, 43, 52, 202
Bonding, 202
  contact, 190
Brace training
  defined, 187
Broad jump
  anticipation, 109
  centered jumping, 109
  distance to be jumped, 106

foundational training, 106
initial configuration, 106
problem—cutting Jump's corner, 111
problems—walking on Jump, 109
teaching method, 106
teaching sequence, 106
Burned-out, 202

Canadian Kennel Club (CKC), 202
Canine abuse, 44
Carryover effect, 202
Challenge the dog, 202
Choke collar, 202
Classical conditioning, 202
Collar tab, 37, 47, 202
Commands
  defined, 202
  let go of object, 33
  Stay, 85
Communication, 202
Competition, 202
  conditioning, 150
  drop on Recall, 63
  gimmicks, 192
Competition showing
  a mini fun match, 149
  AKC Obedience titles—Companion Dog (CD), 140
  AKC Obedience titles—Companion Dog Excellent (CDX), 140
  AKC Obedience titles—overview, 138
  AKC Obedience titles—rules booklet, 140

Pinch collar, 205
Play toy, 205
Play work, 205
Praise, 205
Pressure, 205
Put down, 205

Rapport, 43–44, 205
Recall over Bar Jump, teaching, 92
Recall subterfuge, 50, 51
Recall, the
    characterized, 205
    variants, 12–13
Reinforcement, 205
Reinforcement techniques
    conceptual enhancements, 11–15
    distraction proofing, 3
Release cue, 205
Replacement, 32, 85, 159, 205
Resistance, 205
Retrieve on flat ground
    command modification, 77
    command to release object, 81, 82
    environmental influences, 77
    Front Retrieve adaptation, 84–85
    incorrect hold of object, 82
    prerequisite, 73
    teaching, final phase, 81–82
    teaching, phase one, 73–74
    teaching, phase two, 75
    teaching, phase three, 77
    throwing the object, 84
    verbal bridge, 75
Retrieve over High Jump
    competition rules, 103–4
    extra-mile principle, the, 111
    Jump's colors, 104
    measurement conditioning, 104
    prerequisites, 102
    teaching, 102–3
Retrieving
    "Out!" is not a signal, 82
    aborted retrieve, 115
    attitude, your pet's, 69–70
    attitude, yours, 71
    equipment, 73
    heightening the drive to hunt, 85–87
    over a scaling wall, 115
    pre-training, 71–73
    subtle compulsion, 71
    use of Stay commands, 85
Ring nerves, 205
Ring-wise, 205
Rules of technique (off-leash training)
    clarification, 54
    collar tab, 47–48
    extra-mile principle, the, 111
    multiple leashing, 48–50
    quick hitter, 54
    recall subterfuge, 50–51

throw chain, 47
unapparent control, 51–52

Scaling wall
    conditioning, 115
    conditioning and teaching, 115
    configuration, 111
    Retrieving, 115
Scent Retrieving
    rapport teaching method, 118–19
    Seek-Back, the, 119–21
    structured teaching method, 119–24
    variations, 124–26
Schutzhund, 205
Seek-Back, 119–21
Send-Aways
    AKC application—targeted method, 128–30
    AKC Utility vs. Schutzhund, 127–28
    competition commands, 128
    perspective, 132
    problems and solutions, 130
    Schutzhund applications, 131–32
Show lead, 48, 206
Sit from Motion, 58–59
Sneak-biter, 180, 206
Socialization, 206
Spillover effect, 51, 206
Stimulus, 206
Stress, 206
Submissive, 206
Sweet-and-sour technique
    defined, 206
    illustrated, 194

Teachable moment, 206
Temperament, 206
Temperament testing, 206
Throw chain, 47, 206
Trainable, 206
Trainer, 206
Training, 206
Training equipment
    collar tab, 47–48
    Light lead, 48
    Light line, 48
    Throw chain, 47
Training professionally
    minuses, 182–83
    obligations, 193
    pluses, 183–86
Tricks, kiss, 102

Undercorrection, 44
Utility, 206

Verbal bridge, 48, 75, 159, 206

Willingness, 206
Withers, 206
Work concept, 206
Working, 206